FIRSTCLASS
MARRIAGE

Relationship Lessons from Life on the Road

SVEN ZIMMER

Published by Zimmer Aerogistics
Maitland, FL

First Edition

Library of Congress Control Number: 2014912806
ISBN-13: 978-1500538095

ISBN-10: 1500538094

CONTENTS

DEDICATION

I dedicate this book to the love of my life, Amy, and our two beautiful boys, Luke and Logan. You guys are the inspiration for this book, as I can't imagine anything more precious than a life with you. My hope is that you two boys will be able to look at your mom and I one day and want that kind of relationship in your own lives. Marriage is hard work, especially in this type of profession, but I want you guys to know that no matter where I am in the world, you two and your mom are always in my heart. Honey, you are the rock in our relationship, and our two boys are the luckiest kids to have you as their mother, as I am the luckiest guy to share my life with you. Thanks for being who you are. I love you.

Preface

"People do not get married planning to divorce. Divorce is the result of a lack of preparation for marriage and the failure to learn the skills of working together as teammates in an intimate relationship."

Gary Chapman

It's almost midnight, and the jumbo jet has nearly exhausted all of its fuel, flying for the last 15 hours. The landing lights illuminate the clouds in front of the windshield, and the occasional lightning flash is almost blinding to the three pilots. They lower the gear, extend the last notch of landing flaps and begin their final approach. The rain is getting louder now and the wipers are placed on their highest setting. Finally, about 100 feet above the ground, the exhausted pilots see the bright lights identifying the runway. Moments later, the plane smoothly touches down. After a short taxi to the gate, the Captain shuts down the engines, and for the first time in eight days, it's time for all three pilots to go home.

One of the pilots will return to his lovely home where his wife and three beautiful kids are asleep. He will quietly sneak into bed and look forward to being home with the family for a

1

few days. The other two pilots will go home to find their mailbox overflowing, grass desperately needing a trim, and spoiled milk in the fridge. This is actually a best case scenario as most airlines now have nearly seven out of ten pilots who have been previously married, go home to either an empty house or the wife of their second (some even third or more) marriage. How can it be that they can pilot a jumbo across the Pacific Ocean and be responsible for hundreds of lives a day, yet fail to make their own relationships work at home? Is it their personalities, their work schedules, or perhaps just bad luck? I have been listening to the stories of hundreds of individuals involved in all types of relationships, both good and bad. Even though every story has its own circumstances, there are certain elements that are similar. In this book I have attempted to identify common themes that seem to be the main issues in either marital bliss or distress, so that we can learn to manage them better. This is certainly not a "fix all" book. I am not going to tell you what to do or not to do. Some of you are brand new to this career; for you this book is especially important, as you still have many choices ahead of you. For some, this book will be old news, many stories you have already heard, but I hope you will find it interesting as I try to analyze them a little more. Some will read this and feel as if I was writing about you personally. Many of these stories have happened to a lot of people before and will again in the future. My hope is that you can take the positives and apply them to your own life, then take the negatives and ensure they don't happen to you.

Your Investment

If you want to know where to invest your money to make millions, just ask a pilot. We seem to know everything about investing and spend countless hours reading financial newspapers and magazines, coming up with the next foolproof way to make the big bucks. Of course, none of us are actually successful at this. You might as well throw a dart at the Dow Jones Stocks listings and will probably do better taking that approach. Nonetheless, it gives us something to talk about. We compare investments and figure out which ones give the best rate of return, often times a percent or two can make a huge difference over time. What if I told you that one stock could make or lose you 50 percent in one day? Well, your marriage, in many ways, is that stock.

I can't tell you how many guys spend their entire careers worrying about saving enough money for retirement and studying the markets in great detail, and then find themselves losing more than half of the entire sum in a divorce. Your marriage is just like a mutual fund in that it has many elements that make up the fund. Studying these elements can help you better understand the performance of this fund just like the performance of your marriage. So why then do we spend so much time on investments, stock markets, interest rates, money that you really have no control over at all, but the one thing, your marriage, that can lose you more than 50 percent if not kept together, and that you actually control somewhat, you let collapse and deteriorate? If you had a single investment containing half of your money, wouldn't you spend a lot of time familiarizing yourself with that investment? You would monitor its performance often and ensure that things were on track to keep the investment safe.

Here is another analogy to think about. Suppose you took your retirement and life savings and bought an exotic car hoping that, one day, it will appreciate in value. How would you treat this car? Would you drive it recklessly? I would hope that you would do all the preventative maintenance on the car, always keep it clean, and make sure it was running properly at all times. You would do this expecting that it would give you years of joy and satisfaction down the road (and perhaps the occasional thrill ride). Hopefully, you get the point here. I am just trying to emphasize how important it is to maintain and invest your time in your own relationship. Another approach is to invest all the attention and efforts you put into the markets, into making your marriage last. If successful, you could suffer a 50 percent loss of your entire portfolio and life savings and still break even, if not come out ahead of the guy who gets divorced. The guy who divorces would lose at least 50 percent. Plus if in the above scenario you lost 50 percent of your portfolio, it's safe to assume the divorced guy's portfolio also will take a hit. So really, when it comes down to it, your marriage is much more valuable than any fund or investment you could pick in the markets. In fact, the value yields dividends well beyond dollars and cents. Ideally, you keep both your marriage and your portfolio intact, but unfortunately the odds are very much against you these days. Needless to say, the best retirement advice you will ever get is, "Keep your first (and only) marriage intact."

TIMES ARE CHANGING

My grandparents were married for more than 60 years. How many people will be able to say that 60 years from now? Our society has come to accept divorce as commonplace and having step-parents as typical. How can a society go from one extreme to another in less than 100 years? What's so different now than it was then? More importantly than societal norms, I want to focus on us as individuals. This book will not change the society we live in, but perhaps it can make a difference in your life. I want you to read this book with an open mind and not be judgmental. I am not taking sides, and I am also fully aware that there are always two sides to every story. We are not here to figure out the right and wrong of relationships, but more to discover what works and what doesn't. Sometimes it's the little things that make the biggest changes in our lives.

Most importantly, this is your book; these are your stories, and ultimately, it's all about your own future. It's not about me telling you what is right or wrong. What works and what doesn't. Look at this book as a sign at an intersection from where many roads start. The sign can point to the destination, but it never tells you what the road will be like along the way. Life would be boring if we knew that part anyway. However, with that being said, if you know that one of the roads ends at a cliff, you would take another road. These stories are real, but I changed the names for anonymity. Nonetheless, these individuals went through what you are about to read. This is your book and my hope is that you read this so that you might learn from the mistakes of others and focus on the things they did right, apply it to your own relationships, hopefully beat the odds and live happily ever after.

FOCUS

You are where you are today because of your personality. You are determined, focused, and motivated to accomplish what you set out to do; otherwise, you would have quit the pursuit of this career a long time ago. You were focused for a long time on this moment, finally finding your dream job. Instead of letting go of your motivation to reach this goal, try to redirect that same motivation to your personal life now. You have spent the last few years learning and studying, often times learning from the mistakes of others. If your training partner did a long, cross-country flight and violated a busy airport's airspace, you certainly wouldn't copy his flight plan and make his same mistakes. So you learn and try to improve. That's what we do in life, in general. If you touch a door handle and it burns your hand, you will hopefully either not touch that handle or grab a mitt first and then touch it. Sounds simple, doesn't it? Even my 3-year-old understands this concept. So why then do some of your friends enter doomed marriages that certainly will end up in a divorce? Why do we get married without taking premarital counseling courses to learn from others and apply it to our own marriage? Think about how many people in your life that have been divorced. Are your parents divorced? Have you been in a wedding that ended badly? Have your siblings been divorced? Of those who are not divorced yet, how many relationships do you know that are on the brink of collapse or where one or both partners are miserable? How many married couples are staying together only for the kids, planning to split up once the kids are out of the house? I fly with guys all the time that are miserable in their marriages, and it's a shame to hear how they speak about their partners back at home. I can only imagine what their spouses say about them while they are out of town.

Mahatma Gandhi said, "It is unwise to be too sure of one's own wisdom. It is healthy to be reminded that the strongest might weaken and the wisest might err." No matter how comfortable we get in an airplane, we are always prepared for the worst. Complacency has no place in the flight deck and to ignore mistakes others have made is simply foolish. Most accidents happen to highly qualified crews. So if it happens to them, what keeps that from happening to you? This book focuses on learning from the experiences of others, some good, some bad. We are not judging anyone; the past is the past and that is not something you can change. The future, however, is what you can put in motion today, and learning from others will help guide you to make the right choices.

> *"Wise men learn by other men's mistakes, fools by their own."*
>
> *H.G. Brown*

INTRODUCTION

Love is patient, love is kind. It does not envy, it does not boast, it is not proud. It is not rude, it is not self-seeking, it is not easily angered, it keeps no record of wrongs. Love does not delight in evil but rejoices with the truth. It always protects, always trusts, always hopes, always perseveres. Love never fails. But where there are prophecies, they will cease; where there are tongues, they will be stilled; where there is knowledge, it will pass away.

Corinthians 13:4-8

It's exactly 8:30 p.m., and I've just finished the bedtime routine with my 3-year-old. We brush teeth, hop in bed with a book that he gets to pick out, and read together. Then we turn the lights out, turn on the little turtle that illuminates the ceiling with stars and a moon, and I tell him a story. His favorite stories are of a magic train that travels to lands filled with candy and trucks. Lastly a quick song, a final kiss on his forehead, and its night-night time. I grab my bags, kiss my wife goodbye, and off I drive to the airport. I have a nice used truck, and the drive to the airport is about 45 minutes. Stopped at the red light, I look at my phone to check the latest weather for the places I am flying this trip. Right as the light turns green, I see out of the corner of my eye a car flying though the intersection, clearly not paying attention to the red light. Whoa, that was close. Had I been driving up to the red light and continued once the light turned green I would have certainly been in a direct collision course with the red light driver.

The rest of the drive, I began thinking about my near disaster and how the crash would have hurt me. Would the airbags deploy since it would have been a side impact? Would the glass from the windows cut my eyes, blinding me for life? I started to think about all of the safety features my truck had, all of the technology and research automakers have put into the models year after year. Think about how far safety features have come over the past 20 years alone. Some cars even have the ability to stop all by themselves if they sense an impending impact.

A Typical Commute to Work

I get to the airport and check in for my flight, meet the crew and it's off to work. On the plane, I see an aviation magazine lying on one of the seats and so with nothing else to do at the moment, I grab it and start flipping through it. The issue was about aviation safety and toward the back had an entire section that listed all the accidents for the year, including their causes and the number of fatalities. It's interesting how fatalities affect an individual. You can read about a crash that killed 300 people, but not be affected by it as much as reading about a crash that killed two, if you knew one of them. A recent crash affected me personally, as I knew the first officer well and had even seen the captain around the operations area a few times. Having that personal connection with losing someone you actually know changes how you process the loss. Each one of the crashes listed in the back of the magazine affects thousands of lives, especially for those who lost loved ones. Each crash gets carefully analyzed, the voice recorders are found and examined, the flight data recorders are studied, and in the end, a report is published. This report basically gives, in detail, the causes of the crash and recommendations as to how to prevent this from reoccurring again. Aircraft manufacturers then take these findings into consideration when designing new airplanes and, in some instances, will issue changes that the aircraft operator must adhere to for existing airplanes.

I land at my airline's main hub and have about three hours before my next flight to my home base. It's the middle of the night; I am tired and ready to lie down. After all, I have been up all day with the kids, trying to give my wife a last chance to do her own thing in peace and quiet without dealing with the little rascals. Fighting to stay awake, we finally board the flight. Tonight there are three flights headed up to my base at the same time, so you usually just "eenie meenie miney mo" it and hope it doesn't get delayed or have a mechanical issue. Of course, if something can go wrong, it usually does, so not only does my plane break, they decide to switch the flight numbers assigned to each plane, which requires us to go back inside, list for the new flights, and hope when it's all said and done we get seats up to work. Stress that I really don't feel like dealing with at 3 a.m., but I have gotten used to it, so I just roll with the punches. Luckily, it all works out, and the next thing you know, I am lying on the floor of the freighter plane, cocooned in a blanket so I don't freeze. But I am a happy camper because I am headed to where I work. I think to myself what a high price this is to live where I do, but that's the choice I made, and I will live with it. My eyes get heavy now, and I finally fall asleep.

"HI HONEY, HOW ARE THE KIDS?"

The six-hour flight goes by quickly and soon we are descending into the frozen tundra of Alaska. Nothing beats being dead tired, having slept a few hours on the floor, and then opening the aircraft door to a wall of ice cold air that instantly freezes your nose hair. I left my house more than 15 hours ago, so my family by now has been up for a few hours already. Before I can dial my wife's number to let her know I landed safely, I get a text message from her, a video. I'm excited because occasionally I get a nice video of my kids playing around or doing something silly; those always brighten my day. My favorite video I have ever received was when she filmed my oldest boy's first steps, I have never been more proud of him (see all the things we miss in life while away from home?). I hit play and see that it's a view of my baby boy in his car seat, screaming bloody murder. The camera pans to the right and I see my 3-year-old in his car seat also screaming just as loud, if not louder. Then I hear my wife in the background saying, "Hi dada, wish you were here, we miss you." So much for the silly video of my kids jumping on the couch or building a fort under a blanket. I just spent hours on the floor of a cargo plane, middle of the night flying a few thousand miles away from home just to get to work, and this is the video I get? My motivation to dial her number has just gone from a lot to a negative number, but I call her anyway. Instead of telling her that I was tired from the commute, I am going to stick with the sympathetic and empathetic husband role, making the conversation about her. You think she is going to feel bad for me because I am a little tired, while she is at home dealing with two sick kids who have kept her up most of the night? The conversation is quick, both kids didn't sleep well and they are on the way to the doctor to see if they both have an ear infection. I tell her to call me right after and let me know what the doctor says. Then I head to the hotel for a well-deserved rest before heading out to fly across the ocean.

I arrive at the hotel and spend a few minutes trying to arrange the curtains so that no sunlight shines into my room. I lay down but the second my head hits the pillow, I hear the cleaning staff vacuuming the hallway. So I get up, dig through my suitcase to find earplugs and lie down again. Wait; with earplugs in, I may not hear my phone alarm later. So, lights back on, call the front desk and arrange a call to make sure I get up. Finally, I feel like I can go to sleep. The second my mind drifts off to never land, my phone vibrates and it's my wife. The youngest is just fighting a cold, but the 3-year-old indeed has a double ear infection. My 3-year-old also has a tendency to vomit when he has a fever, so on the way to the doctor, he threw up all over himself and the car. So now she is trying to figure out how to get him home without making a bigger mess. The baby was hungry and hates driving in the car, so of course he is screaming out of pure anger. We hang up, and I once again, try to go to sleep. But with all that stress, my mind is now racing again, and I reflect back to the past 15 hours.

How would my life be different had I had been hit by that car running the red light? What if my flight would have been cancelled? How is my wife handling the stress of dealing with two sick kids by herself? Is she getting tired of being on her own half of the month? Is she thinking that I am gone too much? Is she happy in this marriage? The list goes on and before I know it, I have gone through every scenario possible and still haven't slept. I think of how many crews I have flown with that have been through this before in their marriages, how more than 50 percent of them ended in a divorce. "Eventually, the alarm goes off, and I didn't even know that I actually slept nine hours. I check the time and it's after bedtime for the kids, so I call home real quick and check to see how my family is. My wife sounds exhausted and is clearly ready to go to bed. She then asks me how my commute was and if I got any sleep. Hmm, now what? Should I tell her exactly what I went through to get to work?

EMPATHY

This is the point in our career where we have to realize that we live in parallel worlds. Although we are away from home, life goes on without you being there. Your partner has their workload literally doubled since you are not there to help. We will examine some stories later in this book but the spouse who stays home is doing the hardest job of all, and alone, at that. So being supportive and understanding is key here, just to listen and try to emphasize with what is going on while you are gone. Showing your spouse that you fully support her and making her feel appreciated goes a long way. But this is not a time to make her feel bad for you and your long day. When I interviewed numerous ex-wives, here is what they said regarding this subject:

- "I know my husband is tired commuting to and from work, I know that. But I am the one up all night with the kids, and there is never a dull moment throughout the day."

- "The few minutes I have while my kids are sleeping I want to relax and just sit in peace, not hear about my husband's long night."

- "It's not that I don't care, but I just don't want to hear about it when I am so tired and stressed myself."

So there you have it, your spouse already knows you are tired, so don't expect empathy from home during times like these. Tell the person you are flying with instead, because most likely they went through similar stress getting to work and will be more likely to show you the understanding that you are seeking. Don't get me wrong; I am not telling you to never tell home what you are doing or feeling, just choose the timing wisely.

Why am I telling you all of this? Well to start with, I am getting your attention because I know that this story will sound very familiar to most of you, especially you commuters. But most importantly, I want to focus on the part of the story where I question how my wife is handling this. More than half of the marriages in the United States end in divorce, and for us in the transportation industry, the rate is even higher. This also applies to business people who travel frequently for a living. Think of all the safety features in your car. Most are there as a result of crashes in the past. How many people died who would not have, had their car contained air bags? Remember the days when kids were not required to sit in car seats? How many died because of that? How many planes crashed because they lacked safety features that are standard today? Bottom line: we learn from past accidents and events and try to come up with ways to prevent them from happening in the future. Almost every safety feature in your car is a result of a previous accident, which leads automobile manufacturers to add it. So now reflect back to when you got married. Did you study numerous divorces and analyze what went wrong, then try to implement ways to make sure it doesn't happen to you? Learn from these stories. This is your opportunity to not make the same mistakes others have. It's a freebie, a "Whew, that was a close one, glad it wasn't me" moment. These stories happened to really smart people that have a lot more experience than we do. If it happened to them, it can happen to us.

Seat Mate

I am sure you have noticed that when you are flying as a passenger, the person sitting next to you is sometimes a self-appointed life counselor. They are yours, and you are theirs. In a matter of a few hours, you go from never meeting this stranger next to you to knowing all about his or her life. I think the reason for this is because you are not going to judge them since you don't even know them, and similarly they feel safe to share their life story with you. On top of that, they will tell you things the way they want you to hear them, so they can turn anything into something that may not necessarily be the truth but that makes them feel better about themselves. For that matter, they could make up an entire life and you wouldn't know any better. It's an escape from reality. I never thought that a simple two-hour plane ride could be a ticket to living a completely new life, one where you make up everything you ever wanted. Ever wanted to be a Hollywood stunt actor or a movie producer? Just book a ticket and tell the person next to you that you are. They will not know any better.

In the airline industry, it's much the same, as we are away from home nearly half of our lives, and so we rely on the people we work with for family or support. In the cockpit, we spend hours and hours next to coworkers, who, like yourself, are away from home. It's a known fact that unless you really know whom you are working with, never discuss politics or religion with them. So we talk about what is most dear to us, our toys, boats, planes and new fishing rods... just kidding. We talk about family, kids, spouses, etc. When things are tough at home, we discuss that too. I have spent more than 15 years listening to people's stories about their lives, both good and bad. At the company I work for, the divorce rate is more than 75 percent, meaning the majority of pilots have been divorced at least once. Are you kidding me? Most of these pilots are extremely intelligent, have remarkable backgrounds and are the nicest people. Many of these pilots have fought in wars defending their country, flown at speeds faster than sound in parts of the world I can't even pronounce. How is it that these amazing individuals can accomplish so much but yet fall victim to another divorce? Is it really that difficult? Why do some stay married their entire lives, yet others in the same profession get divorced after 30 years? I may be going out on a limb here, but I consider most of us in the industry to be very intelligent individuals. Can it really be that more than 75 percent of us make horrible decisions when picking a spouse?

This book is comprised of stories, your stories. It's the back of that magazine I was reading on my way to work where all the accidents were listed. These are your marriages that went wrong, and more importantly, marriages that went right. What can we learn from stories that have a happy ending, and how can we apply them to ourselves to ensure our own happy ending? We enjoy all the safety benefits in new cars and fly around in fancy planes with the latest safety equipment installed, but all of this is because manufacturers have learned from the past and from others. Why not do the same in our own personal lives? We spend hours and a lot of money with our retirement accounts to make sure we have enough money to retire. The best retirement plan is to stay married. So why not spend a little time to ensure that we are on track? My grandfather used to always say in his old voice, "I don't have any money, but I have lots of time." This is your life, and only you can change it for the better or worse. You obviously are willing to put some time into this; otherwise you wouldn't be reading this book. This book will hopefully make a difference in your life, and if I can reach just a single relationship, my time was well spent writing this book.

"Learn all you can from the mistakes of others. You won't have time to make them all yourself."

Alfred Sheinwold

CHAPTER 1
To Move or Not To Move

*"God grant me serenity
To accept the things I cannot change,
The courage to change the things I can,
And the wisdom to know the difference."*

Dr. Reinhold Niebuhr

Jim was the starting linebacker for his high school's varsity football team and loved to stay fit. His dad was a farmer in Kansas and worked very hard to support his family. He was raised on that farm and taught Jim the traditional values of being a provider for the family. Jim had always dreamed of being a fighter pilot and early on had his sights set on the Air Force Academy. It was his driving force throughout school and kept him in line to study hard and stay out of trouble. Graduating at the top of his class, he was accepted to the Academy and his dreams of becoming a fighter pilot were becoming a reality. He did well in training and landed a fighter jet slot. Life was good.

Right when he thought things couldn't get any better, he met the girl of his dreams. She was the same age as Jim and was the most beautiful person he had ever met. They started to date, at first casually, but then quickly turning into something more serious. Spending most of their time at either his place or hers, they decided they would move in together to save money. His fondest memory of that time was sitting on a swing by the creek near their apartment, arm in arm, under the moonlight all cuddled up. He confessed his love to her and asked her for her hand in marriage. It was the happiest time of his life, and he couldn't imagine anything better than to have the opportunity to spend the rest of his life with her. They married, bought a nice house, and were truly happy together.

New Beginnings

Like many other military pilots, once his full time commitment was nearing its end, he began to look for employment in the civilian world. At the time, most airlines were not hiring, but a few of the smaller carriers were still looking for pilots. He applied and was happy to get an offer to fly for a carrier that was small but had a lot of opportunity to expand. The only downside was that he would have to commute half way across the country to get to work, and since he was still flying part time in the military, moving was not an option. His wife was excited about his new job, although it now meant that he would be gone much more since he would be commuting to a full time job, as well as still flying at home in the military. But she figured that she had dealt with him being gone for a good part of their lives anyway, so how much worse could it really get? Shortly after he began training, their first child was on the way, and they were happy to begin a new chapter in their family life. It wasn't long before the second child arrived as well. Jim was a proud father to both his little boys.

He tried his best to be present for most special occasions but of course he missed many of them due to being on longer trips or just commuting back and forth to work. Having met his wife in college and before having a real flying job, this was the only lifestyle that they knew. His wife was happy taking care of things at home, and he was doing what he always dreamed of doing, and getting paid for it. He joined the airline when they were still pretty small, so when they expanded and grew to be an international airline, he became more senior and upgraded to captain. His seniority went from fairly good and being home more, to not so good and being gone more, especially over holidays. His pay increased significantly, but his bills seemed to keep up with his raise. His wife did not like the new schedules, but the extra money meant it was easier to run the family finances and to put more money away than before.

The airline soon grew even more and opened a new pilot base in Alaska. Liking the idea of being more senior there since not many people wanted to move, he put his bid in for Alaska. His wife was very established where they lived now and had many close friends she relied on for support when Jim was away on trips. She felt that she was part of the community, a place where she felt comfortable. She liked the idea of Jim being home more, but over the years she had gotten used to it and his presence wasn't really missed. It's not that she didn't miss him or want him home. The fact was that he was gone a lot and she did what she had to in order to not feel lonely. Her friendships made that lifestyle possible. It was her life, and she was happy with it the way it was. So the idea of now leaving all of that behind and moving to Alaska did not seem too appealing to her, even though she knew it would mean Jim not having to commute. Jim, being raised in a traditional home, firmly believed that the man in the house made the ultimate decisions. So with that mentality, he decided on behalf of his family that they would move to Alaska.

LET'S PACK UP AND MOVE

His family was about to be uprooted and move thousands of miles away from what had been their home for years. The kids would have to say goodbye to long time friendships and make new ones up in Alaska. Jim, however, was excited because living in base would mean no more commuting. He was so busy working that he never found time to make any friends where they lived now; so leaving was nothing for him. He could soon simply drive to and from work, what a simple concept. If he was out on a long trip and was delayed on the last leg home, it wouldn't matter. Before, Jim would always plan his commute to the exact second, run every possibility through his head and determine every angle to get home the fastest. Now, that wouldn't be necessary.

I understand Jim's commuter lifestyle, as I am based in Alaska and live in Florida. I sometimes take four flights home, if it means getting home two hours earlier rather than taking two flights and arriving later. I will spend hours in the hotel on the last day of my trip, planning all options to get home. Then

I'll wake up before show time and have a notification that I am two hours delayed. Now, suddenly, the hours worth of work are worthless and there's only a short time to come up with a new plan before heading out the door. We all do this, and for those of us flying internationally, we spend hundreds of dollars a year on Internet and international roaming charges to research and list on flights.

But now, back to Jim in Alaska. He retired from the military when his family moved to Alaska, and Jim, was happier to be working only one flying job. For him the move to Alaska was the right decision, and he had hoped that would hold true for the rest of family, too. A few years passed before he began to notice that his wife had started to distance herself from him. The change was gradual, but noticeable. He noticed that their physical relationship was also much less than the years before and sometimes, it even felt obligatory. He went on trips and heard people talk about their relationships and how many of them had gone through divorces. He started to become paranoid and was trying his hardest to be home more to work on his marriage. Being rather paranoid, he started to wonder if she was having an affair. A few of his colleagues who told similar sounding stories ended up discovering that their wives had been unfaithful. After talking to a few friends in similar situations, he installed a computer monitoring software that tracked keystrokes and took periodic screen shots of the computer screen. He went out on his next trip and sure enough, his suspicions were validated. She was having an affair with one of their close friends who was also married. So he came home and confronted his wife. She told him that she no longer loved him and that she wanted a divorce. They grew apart and she no longer felt any connection with him. Not only did she not love him, but she hadn't loved him ever since they moved to Alaska a few years prior. Jim's world suddenly was turned completely upside down. He went from being happily married in his mind to being another statistic among his colleagues. His kids were almost fully-grown, so they were okay with the separation, but Jim was absolutely crushed. Jim's wife filed for a divorce, received half of all their assets, and afterward the guy she was seeing divorced his wife and they ended up getting married.

Sound familiar? I am willing to bet that you know a few people who have been in similar situations. Jim was left picking up the pieces of his life, and finding himself in such a dark place. He thought back to every scenario they had been through in their lives together and wondered what he could have done differently. What once was a world he was so happy in was now one in which he could not find peace and comfort. Was it the move to Alaska that caused all of this? Or were there underlying issues that would have led to the same result no matter where they lived? Were the trips he went on too long perhaps? He couldn't help but wonder how all of his decisions could have possibly changed the outcome. Unfortunately, he will never find the reason why life took an irreversible turn for the worse.

EMBRACE YOUR NEW SURROUNDINGS

Rob is a colleague of mine who, under similar circumstances, moved his entire life from Atlanta to Alaska to live where he was based. He has a lovely wife Jane, three young children, and he came up the civilian ranks to land his dream job at the major airlines. However, Rob was based in Alaska, just like Jim. After commuting for the first few years at this new job, they decided to move to Alaska on a trial basis to see how they would like it. They rented a nice house and the kids went to the local school, quickly adapting to their new surroundings and making lots of new friends. Jane was a part-time teacher in Atlanta; so having experience, she applied to work as a substitute teacher at her children's school. After taking some exams to transfer her license, the school offered her a part-time position, and she worked on occasion at the school. Rob was pretty junior in seniority, but that also meant that many of his trips were short. He would leave for a quick four-day trip, be home for four-days, and then out again. Most senior guys hated this type of schedule because of the difficult commute. Even though Rob worked a lot, he was home regularly, which made it seem much more tolerable.

After a year or so, a full time position at the school opened up, and Jane was chosen to fill that spot. Jane was now very involved in the school. She worked normal hours while the kids attended class, and made lots of new friends. The next thing you know, three years passed by and Rob and Jane were busier than ever. Between sports for the kids and outdoor activities with friends and neighbors, they barely had down time. Rob continued to fly the short trips and was able to manipulate his schedule where he could pick the days he wanted to be home, usually weekends. The airline that Rob was working for eventually started to grow and that meant new positions were open in the lower 48 states. His family could now move back to Atlanta. One night Rob and Jane sat down and discussed their options. Jane was so happy with their new life in Alaska that there was absolutely no way she wanted to move back. She was busier than ever, felt great being in such good shape with all the outdoor activities they were involved in, and had made so many new friends. Life was perfect in her mind; why fix what's not broken? Today, it's been nearly eight years and they are still happier than ever living in Alaska.

LONELY

So what's the difference here between Jim and Rob's lives? Both moved their families to a state many miles away from home, one got divorced and the other is living happily ever after. Jim's wife was very close to her family and had her own little life set up the way she liked it. Friends filled the void her husband left when he was away flying. Many of her friends were in similar situations since their husbands were away flying in the military too. They all knew what the other was going through, so they could support each other well. When Jim's family moved to Alaska, all of the key elements that made their lives function were missing. There were no more friends to come over and fill that void. When Jim was home, everything was fine. The family was complete, but that was only temporary. The minute Jim walked out that door, his life on the road was as usual. Every time he was home things appeared fine, his wife seemed to be happy. But for his wife, the time during which Jim was gone was miserable. Her kids had grown and become more and more independent. She missed the support of her friends and even more so her family. Sure, she made new friends, but what did they know about being alone for half the month? Feeling sad and alone, depression soon followed and things became worse every time Jim would leave.

Jim's wife had always loved horses. He thought maybe that would cheer her up. They built a barn on their land and bought a horse. This cost a lot of money, and since Jim hated debt, he would pick up trips to pay for the increased expenses. This meant that he was gone even more, and the horse became a symbol of her being alone even more in her eyes. They sold the horse and decided it would be cheaper to rent one occasionally at a barn close by. A very nice lady who befriended Jim's wife ran this barn. She traveled often and could use all the help with the horses while away for work, so Jim's wife was glad to help out. Now she had a purpose again and felt needed. The ladies' husband also liked horses and would often times help out at the barn when Jim's wife was stepping in for his wife's absence. So here she was at the barn, at a place where she had purpose, felt needed, and now another man was showing her attention. Can you see where this story is going next? Jim's wife ended up leaving Jim for this man.

Accountability

Rob's wife Jane, on the other hand always had purpose. She stayed busy, and he made sure he was home enough to show her the attention she needed. They became involved in the community, which was a source of accountability for her. In Thomas Stanley's book, *The Millionaire Mind*, he writes, "I think success really involves the situations you get yourself into and the people you meet. It's the relationships that you develop with the people around you." Jane chose to surround herself with good people who kept her accountable, work or activity-wise. Had Jim's wife gone out and made new valuable friendships, kept active in the community, or taken advantage of some of the many outdoor activities Alaska has to offer, things might have been different.

I understand that this is not for everyone, and that's why we must search within ourselves to determine if such a move if feasible. For myself, for example, I sat down with my wife and discussed all the options. She is very close with her family, involved in our community, and is simply happy where she is. My kids are established in school, have their friends, and are doing great. So why would I uproot them and make them move to a new state? I bite the bullet every month and commute to work, not because I love commuting, but because I know that it is much easier to uproot myself every time I have to go to work than it would be to uproot the rest of my family. But that's just my family and me. You need to determine what's best for you and your family. Rob and Jane would make the move over again any day; whereas Jim would have never left his home, if he could do it over again. Remember that your spouse is home the entire month, while you are gone for half of that time. Having a happy spouse at home is worth more than I can explain. It's up to you, as a couple, to determine what price you are willing to pay for that.

CHAPTER 2
Bigger Isn't Always Better

"We are all dreaming of some magical rose garden over the horizon - instead of enjoying the roses that are blooming outside our windows today."

Dale Carnegie

Mike was an A student in high school and was very involved in all of the sports the school had to offer. He loved to stay in shape and lead his teammates. He was well respected and regarded as a great team captain. He was the youngest of three boys, and he grew up in a beautiful, small home with his parents and his brothers. During his last few years of high school, his mother really wanted to upgrade the kitchen, but Mike's father, who had always tried to live very frugally and within their budget, said they could not afford it. She was fully determined and set on doing the renovation, and so the arguments began and progressively got worse. Believe it or not, they ended up getting a divorce during Mike's senior year. 28 years down the drain for a kitchen remodel. The divorce hit Mike hard; he had never imagined his parents living apart, something he promised to never let happen to himself. This planted a seed in Mike's mind, something that would come to haunt him later in life.

When he graduated high school, he joined the Naval Academy and became a pilot. He didn't have the passion for aviation like most of his classmates, but it quickly grew on him and the idea of blowing things up while flying fast was exciting. His flight training progressed very well. He was always very studious and spent most of his free time either working out or at the local library studying. One day when he was studying there, he met a young college student who sat across from him at the table. Finding her very attractive, Mike started basic small talk quietly, and the next thing he knew, he was having coffee with her. Kathy was her name and she was from a small town in South Dakota. She was enticed by him being in the Navy and never imagined dating a fighter pilot in her wildest dreams. Kathy grew up in a family of five, just like Mike, but her parents were still happily married. Her dad worked long hard hours and they appeared to be very well-off judging by their lifestyle. Money was never really an issue, if they wanted something, they would buy it. Growing up, the kids always had the latest and greatest toys; her mom and dad were driving new cars, and the house appliances were always the latest models. If they had money, they spent it, which seemed to be the family motto.

KEEPING UP WITH THE JONESES

Mike and Kathy spent every free minute together and quickly their romance blossomed. Mike and Kathy lived together and after the Academy moved into a small little house that was just the right size for them. Kathy was very active in the Officer Wives Club and had a lot of great friends she would do things with while Mike was out flying. The other women became part of her extended family, and when Mike was deployed for months at a time, they were all she had. Not only for her, but also for them was this society a wonderful support network that she greatly treasured.

This society of course came with strings, jealousy being a big drama topic among the women. One would receive a romantic love letter from her husband and would read it to the other ladies, and then of course they all wanted the same for themselves. When the men came home after being away on the ship, they would usually bring home nice gifts, sometimes even fancy jewelry. Excitedly, the wives would then show off their new piece of jewelry to the other women, and although happy for each other, they couldn't help but feel envious. Quickly, the "Keeping up with the Joneses" was a huge deal and it seemed to be like a game where they would each try to top one another. This of course, led to cat fights and drama among the women in the club, often times resulting in the group being split into sides. The drama would soon carry over to Mike and Kathy's marriage, and they would argue late into the night about spending and budgeting.

Mike learned from his dad to live frugally, live within your means and save as much as possible. Kathy, on the other hand, grew up spending freely and never had to budget much of anything. If there was something she wanted, she would buy it and tell Mike about it afterward, completely opposite of what

Mike was used to growing up. The fights got worse over time and placed a great strain on their marriage. For Kathy, living within a budget meant not being able to keep up with everyone else and that was something she had never had to face and certainly not something she wanted to start.

Mike did his military flying tours and eventually began the process of applying to all the various airlines that were hiring. His buddies did the same, and quickly one after another received job offers from big airlines. Mike, however, for some reason never received an interview call. He was starting to get pretty depressed about why he wasn't getting calls. The wives club ladies would announce who got what job and how much they would be making and so forth; Kathy put on a great act to appear happy for them but deep inside was dying for her to be able to tell them Mike had landed a great job, too. Then finally one day, a cargo company called Mike and offered him a job. They were a small outfit and flew mostly old equipment at night. Not too excited about it, he figured it was better than nothing so after discussing it with Kathy, he accepted the offer and he and Kathy moved just outside the airline's main hub. They bought a nice little house, 2100 square feet and felt that this was a perfect home in which to start raising a family.

Kathy was never a shy woman, so she quickly made a lot of new friends in the neighborhood. Her new circle of friends were lovely and a great support group for each other when their loved ones were away on trips. Most of her friend's husbands also flew for this airline so they were all in the same boat as far as lifestyle and income was concerned. But once again, the "Joneses" factor took shape and the cycle of keeping up started again.

It seemed that no matter how much Mike's paycheck increased, they would spend it all every month. The more he made, the more she spent. Mike, paying most of the bills himself and balancing the checkbooks, saw the money come in and go out. Even though he saw the money matters get worse, he was so afraid to fight with his wife because he saw how that turned out for his parents. His dad did that and it led to his mom leaving, tearing the family apart over money matters. He knew what he needed to do, but was simply too afraid. Meanwhile the airline grew rapidly and Mike's seniority moved up quickly as a lot of new pilots joined the outfit, which were placed below him on the list. The airline also started to buy some more airplanes, which was even better news for Mike. Mike and Kathy decided it was now a good time to start a family, so they had two kids within three and a half years. They had a lovely home with two healthy kids and a good job; Life seemed to be going great.

LET'S BUILD A MANSION

After a few more years, Mike was senior enough to upgrade to Captain and this meant a substantial pay raise. Some of their friends had bought new homes and they all seemed twice the size of Mike and Kathy's home. Kathy was now starting to feel the pressure of keeping up with the rest of her friends; their perfect little house suddenly seemed small. Even though her kids would be leaving home in a few years, she wanted something bigger with perhaps a little land. She had always dreamed of owning her own horse and this could be the perfect opportunity to do so. She knew that the new home would have to be spectacular and top all of her friends' homes. She decided to design the home herself with the help of the top architectural firm in town.

The price tag for the design was approaching ten thousand dollars, and her dream home was finally on paper. It looked beautiful. Mike had been very busy at work flying and so wasn't included or involved in the design phase up to this point. He remembered Kathy talking about a new home and was fine with the idea of upsizing to a bigger one, after all he was making more money and a bigger home with some land would mean he could have a nice little tool shed to work on some projects. Never in his wildest dreams did he imagine what was about to be laid out in front of him: a whopping five bathrooms in a house totaling over 7,800 square feet. Those were the new plans for her dream home. Mike just about had a heart attack right there when he saw the plans. How could they possibly afford such a mansion, and why would they even need to? The plans were ridiculous. What would they need five bathrooms for especially when the kids were out of the house soon?

Kathy had somewhat anticipated his reaction, and to cushion the financial blow, she designed the home to be built in stages, the last few stages Mike would complete himself. This would keep the cost down and allow them to save on some of the construction costs, but still the price tag was outrageous. Mike had always been very handy and good with building things; surely this would be a fun project that he would do on his days off from flying. Kathy wanted Mike to spend half of the month flying around the world and then come home to work full time on building a home. Mike thought this plan was crazy, so he sat her down and told her that it was an insane idea that would surely kill him emotionally and physically. He would have absolutely no free time, would never see the family, and would feel exhausted and overworked. In short, he would hate life. When he saw how upset she became, he quickly backed off since he felt like he was heading down the same road his father did several years prior. Kathy heard Mike's concerns, but continued to push the plans on him, as she was determined to build this house.

Let the Bank Decide

One of the pilots Mike was flying with had a brilliant idea, which Mike set out to do on his next break at home. He would agree to the plans and figured that there was no way in the world the bank would lend such a large amount of money for a house that would only be partially complete. He figured this way the bank would put the fatal arrow in the plans and they would be forced to design a much more reasonable home. Mike would still look like the good guy, an image he had desperately tried to maintain. He figured if he could let Kathy do whatever she wanted, he would keep the family together and happy, an illusion that he created when he saw his parents split up years prior. The fear of losing his wife and family was much greater than any money issues and he would die trying to keep everyone happy, even at the expense of their financial well-being.

After coming home from his next trip, Mike and Kathy went to the bank to present the plans and ask for a loan, a loan bigger than he had ever imagined being liable for. Although a little nervous, he felt confident that his plan would succeed. After all, what banker in their right mind would approve a giant loan for a home partially complete? When they arrived at the bank, he was surprised to learn that Kathy and the female banker shared mutual friends in the community. The banker knew that all of Kathy's friends were upgrading their homes and figured that if they all had good enough incomes, surely Mike would too. The loan was approved, and Mike's worse nightmare had suddenly become a reality. Kathy was happy and couldn't understand why Mike was so upset. She was focusing on how much money they would save by him doing part of the work himself, and if the bank approved them, then they obviously could afford the house. The two left the bank that day, their lives forever changed.

Mike's parent's divorce scared him so much that he was unable to put his foot down to put an end to the crazy house plans. Kathy didn't think twice about the high costs; however, in her defense, she never had to before. Construction began shortly after, marking the beginning of the end for their marriage, as they knew it. Each phase of the construction seemed to run over budget and always took longer than planned. By the time the house was half way done, the money was gone. So now Mike had to go back to the bank and ask for more money. Again, the bank approved the loan since they, too, now had a financial interest in the house's completion.

Before Mike knew it, the time had come for Mike to go to work on the house to finish the rest. The task was daunting and seemed overwhelming. Mike would fly a long trip all over the world and then come home to face the hard labor of building a home. Concrete, woodcutting, painting, it never seemed to end or get any easier. He would finish working on the house late at night after a few days, and then wake up the next morning, put on his uniform, and head to work. Mike was now absent from his life, never really being present even when at home, physically nor emotionally. Not only did his physical health begin to deteriorate, his relationship with Kathy also started taking a turn for the worse. She was busy picking out decor and colors for the house, spending more with money they didn't have, on a house that wasn't even close to being finished.

I'VE HAD ENOUGH

Their two children, now in high school themselves, loved the house. Even though it wasn't finished yet, it was on a big piece of land and had a roof over it. Can you say PARTY HOUSE? So while Mike was away on trips, guess where most of the high school students spent their weekends, only to leave Mike with empty beer cans and garbage to pick up when he came back from his trip? The kids seemed to inherit the spending habits of their mother as well, spending freely and never saving a penny for anything.

Mike didn't know what to do anymore. This house was killing him, and he began to realize that something just had to give. He told his wife that he was drained, exhausted, and feeling at his wits' end. Mike had asked the bank for more money, perhaps they could hire out the rest of the work to finish the home, but overextended now the bank declined. Selling the house as it stood was also not an option. Who would want to buy a half-finished house? Certainly, Mike would have also lost money he invested. Not to mention that Mike was paying a mortgage on his existing home as well as that of the mansion he was working on. It got so bad that he would sleep at the unfinished house for days on end, working sunrise to sunset. This of course took more of a toll on his marriage, to the point where Kathy became used to living alone. Their romantic relationship was all but non-existent. They would talk to discuss house or kid issues, but that was about it.

Their youngest was now about to graduate from high school and was looking at going to college. Facing the additional expense now of that too, Mike finally threw up his hands and called out for mercy. No more, he thought. He could not live this way anymore. This house was taking up all of his time; he was exhausted, living in a loveless marriage, and now facing bankruptcy even though he was making more money than most Americans make. He realized that although his parents got divorced, he still had a good relationship with each one of them, and so he figured that he could do the same with his kids. The cost of keeping his marriage together was simply too great, something he never thought he would say.

THE APPLE DOESN'T FALL FAR FROM THE TREE

Meanwhile, Kathy's parents had run out of money themselves since they never paid attention to their spending. They always spent freely, and now that they were in retirement, they had no more income. Things got so bad that they soon lost their house, forcing them to move in with Kathy. What used to be Mike and Kathy's perfect little home, now became a refugee camp for the free spenders, one that Mike was paying for but not welcome into anymore. Mike and Kathy decided to legally separate, divide their assets and debt, most of it seeming to be the latter. Their oldest daughter also was dealing with debt. She had the IRS garnishing her wages and her credit card bills kept piling up. Mike decided to cut his losses. He would live in the unfinished house until he could sell it, would help his daughter as much as he could, but would not be part of Kathy and her family's financial disaster anymore. Mike, for the first time in years, felt free, a feeling he had forgotten what it felt like.

Looking back at Mike's marriage, it's pretty safe to say that it was doomed from the beginning. Mike and Kathy had come from entirely different backgrounds. Mike was used to living frugally and being financially responsible; Kathy, on the other hand, spent freely and often times well beyond her means. Mike failed to communicate properly with Kathy about finances out of the fear of losing her. The ironic thing is that the very same fear of losing her actually was the leading factor of why Mike did lose her. His fear became a reality, something that perhaps could have been prevented if properly dealt with early on.

Kathy told Mike during the separation process that had he told her that he really didn't want to build the huge house, she would have been ok with that. She figured that if the bank approved it then it must be something they could afford. The hundreds of arguments for years prior about money never really hit home for either of them. Mike was so scared of losing Kathy that he allowed things to get to the point of no return. Kathy learned her spending habits from her mother, then passed that habit down to her own children. As a parent, you lead by example. If your kids see you living a certain way, they will often times adapt to that same lifestyle.

There is an old saying, "Actions speak so loudly that I cannot hear what is being said." Saying something is one thing, but doing it, something entirely different. Just like Kathy's parents corrupted the next two generation's spending habits, Mike's parents corrupted his ability to face and deal with conflict. How you live your life is much more important than what you say. Your children are like sponges and will carefully analyze everything you do in life, often times imitating that behavior in their own lives. The apple doesn't fall far from the tree; there is a lot of truth to that.

THE MORE YOU MAKE, THE MORE YOU SPEND

Mike's story is obviously the extreme case, but I am willing to bet that every one of you reading this book, including myself, have been part of the rat race to keep up with the Joneses. Will Rogers said, "Too many people spend money they earned to buy things they don't want to impress people that they don't like." Stop and think about that for a moment.

When I was hired as a First Officer at a small regional airline, my pay was less than $15,000 a year. Boy, that was a lot of money for me. I was finally rich, I could travel the world for free and had money to spend. I would fly with Captains who were making double what I was making. Unreal, I thought to myself, these guys are super rich. Then you would hear the stories about how broke they were, had no money, and needed to make more. What idiots, I thought, they obviously have no idea how to manage finances at all. I couldn't even begin to imagine if I had twice the pay, I could buy anything I wanted. I specifically remember one Captain telling me, "It doesn't' matter how much you make, the more you make the more you spend." Right, what an idiot, I thought. But wrong I was, big time!

After a few years, I became a Captain and not only did I make more and spend more, I made more and owed more, even worse. But how could this be, how can you spend so much more than before when you had so little? This is not a finance book, so I won't bore you with anymore money stories for now, but trust me when I say to you that you need to be aware of this "spending" phenomena. There are countless books on budgeting and finances, ask some of your friends or colleagues and determine which is best for you, but please do it sooner rather than later. Our jobs are stressful enough as it is, you don't need to add additional stress because of money issues. Still have doubt? Then consider this, the number one cause of divorce in America is money fights and money problems. Get a book, take a class, talk to peers, whatever works, but better to do it now rather than later.

As for Mike, do you think that his wife would have been happy if they actually finished the house and moved in? Had they done so, how long would it have been until the next "new thing" Kathy would have wanted? Dealing with this "Joneses" factor and finances is very much like a diet. Diets come and go, just like budgets and watching what you spend for a month or two. It is the lifestyle and the thought process that will endure the temptations of society and life itself. Only when you change that, will you will actually conquer true financial and material freedom.

What if Mike had sat down with his wife and thoughtfully expressed his concerns for the new house project? What if his wife would have included him more in the design of the house so that Mike would have been in the loop more, having an opportunity to stop things from getting out of hand early on in the process? What if Mike overcame his fears of losing his wife and just trusted that the relationship was strong enough to endure a simple "NO" to her plans? In the end they both ended up with much less than they started, not only financially, but also even worse without each other.

Mike was too concerned about hurting her feelings; yet, if you asked Mike to do it over again, he would say that he would wage great wars and arguments to stop the project during the beginning phases, knowing that the damage would be fixable. The fact that Mike was always working, either on the house or flying, meant he was never around to be part of the marriage. So his wife grew distant and became comfortable without him being around. So much so, that she enjoyed time alone more than the time when he was around. Once this happens, it is difficult to reverse the course, and so it's crucial to never let things get to this point in the first place. The very thing that Mike was afraid of was what ended up happening.

LIVE WITHIN YOUR MEANS

To live within your means is not only about being financially responsible but also crucial to a happy relationship. Bigger is not always better and most people today have confused the definition of being rich. Having fancy cars and a big house doesn't necessarily make you rich at all. In fact, most people that have this are broke. They spend their entire lives making payments to have these extravagant things, never really owning them.

I heard a story where a guy was driving his kid to a birthday party one afternoon. They pulled up to the house, a huge mansion with lots of big new cars in the driveway, and the kid looked at his dad and asked why they were not rich like his friend. His dad stopped the car, turned to his son, and told him that they in fact are much more wealthy than his friend is. The kid seemed confused at first, but then the dad went on to explain to him that they lived in a nice small home, which they owned. The car they were sitting in, also owned. The vacations they would go on were paid for in cash and the gifts they would receive were also paid for with money they saved throughout the year. So what they had, they owned. The kid's friend on the other hand lived in a huge mansion, mortgaged to the hilt, the cars were leased, so basically rentals, and the fancy things they had inside the house were courtesy of Amex and Visa. The kid began to understand and seemed happy with his dad's explanation.

Buying something you actually saved for is much more satisfying than having it and worrying about making the payments. We are all in control of our own happiness and must do our best to not have society take control of that ability. We alone decide what matters to us and what doesn't; often you realize that you have everything it takes to be truly happy. If having a material thing determines your happiness, then you should question if that thing is worth having. Chances are, the moment you get it, you will be looking for the next thing to get. Remember, the more you have, the more you have to worry about.

CHAPTER 3
The Most Sincere Smile

"We are all dreaming of some magical rose garden over the horizon - instead of enjoying the roses that are blooming outside our windows today."

Dale Carnegie

I want to add to the previous chapter, one of the most life changing events in my own life. I feel as if sometimes we get so wrapped up in daily life that we forget how good we all really have it. Living in the present is much more difficult than it appears. Just to give you an example, recently I found myself at Disney World with my two young kids. I was stressed from getting them ready to go to the park, ensuring I had food packed and the diaper bag stocked. The kids were fussy on the drive and now I was battling the heat and crowds in line for a 30-second ride. As we were looking for a place to sit in the shade, we passed a group of kids wearing "Make a Wish" shirts. Entire families wore these shirts, smiling and laughing, having a good time. I immediately started to think that this could be one of those kid's last trip to Disney, or for mater last trip period. Then I saw a dad push a wheel chair with his severely handicapped child in it. Seriously, how lucky am I to have two healthy kids? My stress immediately went away and I was forced to live in the present, for I was reminded how good I truly have it. I was almost ashamed that just a few minutes ago I was stressing about the silliest little things, when people that have "real" stress were walking right next to me.

CAMBODIA

Before my wife and I got married, we decided to travel as much as we could before we settled down and had kids. So we did, and we traveled a lot. Europe, Caribbean, within the United States, Asia, you name it. We had a blast. One of the most memorable places we visited was Siem Reap, Cambodia. This magical city contains the ruins of the old Angkor temples and the entire place is absolutely magical. Having flown in from Bangkok, we felt like we were in a time machine flying from a hustling and bustling city to an ancient village hundreds of years ago.

We checked in to our quaint little bed and breakfast and started planning our temple visits over the next few days. Things are incredibly cheap there and the food is amazing; however, if you are a picky eater, then you might not love it as much as we did (we had no idea what we were eating half of the time, but it was delicious). We spent four days trekking around the old temple ruins and had an amazing time doing so. The last day we decided to hire a car to take us to Kampong Phluk, a village built on stilts in the giant lake called Tonle Sap. It was absolutely incredible to see how people live there. Entire families living in cardboard boxes, children dressed in torn rags running around the streets chasing flies for fun. I could go on with this, but you get the point.

We got on a little boat that barely fits my wife, our guide, and me. As we floated through the village in our little boat, we saw even more poverty and couldn't imagine it getting any worse. But right then, something incredible happened. We passed a beaten down float carrying a structure that somewhat resembled a shack, maybe more of a shelter at that. On the back of that float sat a young lady, maybe early twenties, and she looked at us and just smiled and waved. It was the most genuine and sincere smile that I have ever seen in my entire life. She appeared simply happy, full of life. Maybe she was excited that her new float home was being moved somewhere else, who knows, but she appeared genuinely happy. I thought to myself, how can somebody who has so little be so happy? But then I started to think more about it, realizing that she actually might have everything she could want.

Think about that for a moment. If all you want in life is to have your health, clothes, a basic car, simple home and food to eat, then you might suddenly find yourself having everything you want. You, and only you, are in charge of controlling your desires. Unfortunately, our society has hijacked this ability and we have come to accept the fact that the society we live in controls our wants and needs. Pick up any magazine and you will see ads for the next better and newer item, from cars to clothes to watches, and so on. Wants and illusory needs are placed into our minds and the next thing you know, you are not happy until you get that next thing. But when you get it, a newer one is available and the rat race starts over again.

Ever wonder why you spend more when you make more? More money means you can buy more stuff that you think will make you happy. The more stuff you buy, the more stuff you are worried about losing. You work harder to make more money, then you spend more again, and the viscous cycle continuous. Dr. Schopenhauer said, "We seldom think of what we have but always of what we lack."

THE 10 MOST IMPORTANT THINGS IN YOUR LIFE

If you ever find yourself unhappy but cannot place a finger on what it is that is causing that unhappiness, take a step back and mentally try to strip yourself of everything you posses. Take away everything, not just your material possessions like your car and house, but also all of your senses. Take away your ability to see, smell, hear, feel, and communicate. Take away your limbs, friends, and family; reduce yourself to a simple form of just being alive.

Now start, one by one, adding 10 things that matter most in your life. For example, you might think the first thing you want is your sight back, so that you can see the world and the people you love. Then you might add your sense of smell so that you can taste, perhaps your ears so that you can hear the birds singing. How about a spouse that loves you unconditionally? Then add hands and arms so that you can hold them. Add legs so that you walk through the grass that you can see and pick a flower that you can smell with your new sense of smell. How about the ability to speak so that you can tell your spouse that you love him or her? Now that you have your basics back, how about somewhere to live, maybe a home that is in a safe neighborhood and provides protection from the elements. Then you might want a car, reliable and safe enough for your family. Now you need a job that allows you to buy food for your family, maybe even allow for a vacation once you have saved enough.

You get the point here, you just keep adding the things that matter the most in your life, in order of most importance until you get to 10. Then stop and think about how many of those 10 things you already have in life. Chances are the top 10 most important things in your life are things you already have.

Not bad for a start. Yet we worry and stress about things that don't even truly matter in life, the things that do matter, you usually already have. Now add 10 more, and again you will most likely find that you already have them. The woman on that floating raft might have had all of her top 10 things in life. What else could she possibly ask for? It is not until you fully disconnect yourself from the influences of our society that you realize what you actually have and of that what really matters. Can you imagine what the woman on that float would say if you complained to her about your iPhone being the four and not the five model? How embarrassing would it be if we told her we were stressing about the fact that our power bill for our five-bedroom home was high since we ran the air conditioning all summer long?

Life is relative, and I know that. But when we strip ourselves of all the material possessions we have, we are on a level playing field with any person in the world. If we have our basic health, all of our body parts and all of our senses, we have so much already. Entire generations live in parts of the world with really not much more than that. Many of the things we think we need to be happy are just that, thoughts. The big companies of the modern world are not interested in you finding happiness. In fact, many would go out of business if you were actually content with what you had. They take great pride in manipulating your wants and desires to increase their own bottom line; keep that mind when you find yourself wanting something newer or better. I am not saying to never buy anything new or upgrade to better things at all, but it shouldn't determine whether or not you are happy. "Wealth consists not in having great possessions, but in having few wants." - Epictetus.

If you get anything out of this chapter at all, please let it be that sometimes the things that make you the happiest, are things that you already have, and often, those things are sitting right next to you, you just have to look. Dale Carnegie wrote in his book, *How to Stop Worrying and Start Living*, "About ninety percent of the things in our lives are right and about ten percent are wrong. If we want to be happy, all we have to do is to concentrate on the ninety percent that are right and ignore the ten percent that are wrong."

Remember that you alone are in charge of your own happiness. If you find yourself unhappy, take a step back and think about what it is that you truly desire. You might discover that you actually have more than you thought you had. If the young woman on her floating home can offer a genuine smile and radiate happiness, so can you. It's like the classic 1969 Rolling Stones song, "You can't always get what you want, but if you try sometime, you just might find, you get what you need."

CHAPTER 4
Talk To Me Goose

"A successful marriage is the ability to successfully manipulate conflict, the key to this is communication."

Anonymous Quote from an individual married more than 34 years

On August 14, 2005, a Helios Airways Boeing 737 took off from Larnaca, Cyprus, enroute to Athens, Greece. The flight was under the command of Hans-Jürgen Merten, a 58-year-old German contract pilot hired by Helios for the holiday season. He was assisted by First Officer Pampos Charalambous, 51, a Cypriot who flew for Helios full time. When the flight arrived earlier from London, the inbound crew noticed some strange noises coming from the door seals. Maintenance worked on the seals and part of the maintenance procedure was to place the pressurization system in the manual mode. The work was completed without any unusual findings and the aircraft was cleared to continue service.

When the new crew arrived at the plane to get it ready to fly the first leg to Athens, they completed their preflight checks and passenger boarding commenced. The pressurization panel is checked on three different sections of the preflight checks;

however, on this day for some reason both pilots failed to notice that the system was still in the manual mode from maintenance earlier. Not only was the pressurization system left in the manual mode, the outflow valve was also left open, which is basically like having a small hole in the back of the plane. This hole is normally opened and closed automatically to control the cabin pressurization, but since the system was left in manual, the hole remained opened.

The plane took off and began its climb to cruise altitude; it wasn't long before the pilots received the first warning indication that the cabin pressure was exceeding safe limits. The Captain and the First Officer both spoke very broken English. It was good enough to communicate basic aviation terms and checklists, but too poor to discuss a system. The situation required thinking and speaking outside the box. In this case, a simple discussion about what was happening was not really possible due to the language barrier. Shortly after the first warning indication, the Captain used the radio to contact the ground mechanics that had previously done the work on the pressurization system. The ground engineer asked the Captain to ensure the pressurization system was in automatic mode, but by that time the effects of loss of oxygen had taken its toll and the crew became unconscious. Long story short, the plane continued to climb to cruise, flew for three hours on autopilot, and eventually ran out of fuel and crashed into the hills in Greece killing all 121 on board.

There is of course, more to the crash, but I want to focus primarily on the communication aspect. The pressurization system in manual is not a big deal. Many airplanes can be dispatched to fly with it in manual as long as the crew is aware of it and maintains proper cabin pressure throughout the flight. When the crew received the first warning of cabin pressure exceeding the limits, right then, they should have stopped climbing and started troubleshooting the issue. The language barrier between the Captain and the First Officer was so great that a simple discussion about the state of situation was not possible, resulting in a lack of a common understanding of what was actually happening. Speaking a foreign language is difficult as is, but when you venture out of your knowledge base of that language it can quickly become unintelligible. The fate of the flight would most likely been very different had both crewmembers spoken the same native tongue.

TRIVIALITIES

Why am I telling you this story? It's the basic principle that often, simple communication can make or break a marriage between two people. Sometimes the smallest, simplest little issues are not properly communicated and those issues can be blown way out of proportion or grow into something much more serious. Judge Joseph Sabath of Chicago, after acting as arbiter in more than forty thousand un-happy marriages said, "Trivialities are at the bottom of most marital unhappiness." Former District Attorney Frank S. Hogan also said,

"Fully half of the cases in our criminal courts

originate in little things. Barroom bravado, domestic wrangling, an insulting remark, a disparaging word, a rude action — those are the little things that lead to assault and murder. Very few of us are cruelly and greatly wronged. It is the small blows to our self-esteem, the indignities, the little jolts to our vanity, which cause half the heartaches in the world."

Often, when you actually distance yourself from your situation and analyze things, you will find that really, what you thought was so bad, might not be so bad after all.

Harboring petty things in a relationship can be easier in the spur of the moment than dealing with them, but over time they will usually grow into a much bigger issue than before. I remember my father would work all day at his little retail store, then come home and see the laundry basket full, dishes in the sink, and the trash can full. Instead of telling his wife that it would help him if she made more of an effort to help out with house chores, he would stress out and do all of those things himself. He wouldn't mention it to her and gave her the cold shoulder at night when he was tired and exhausted. His not being talkative or loving at night then hurt her feelings, so she reacted to that by being mad at him for treating her coldly. He would then see her treating him that way, and he would get angry that she didn't appreciate him or all of the things he would do on a given day.

From his perspective, he would work all day, come home to do more work around the house, then get yelled at each night by his wife for not being loving enough. In her mind, she saw him coming home after being gone all day, and all she wanted was a simple hug or kiss to show her that he loved her. The cycle continued until eventually, usually about once a week, a huge fight would erupt where every little thing that had festered in their minds got thrown at the other person. All it would have taken was for him to communicate to her that he was tired from working all day and would appreciate if she helped with the chores. Then this whole mess could have been avoided.

To make things even worse, our personalities are very much like my dad's in this example. We like structure and organization; it's how we operate in a cockpit and comes natural to us. It's not that my dad's wife didn't help around the house, but she just didn't do it on his schedule. In his mind, he was showing her love by doing all the work, but for her, physical touch would have been much more effective. We must learn to communicate our love and feelings in a way that the other person can actually understand. Having the type of personalities that we typically do, it is often difficult to understand why things that need to be done are not being done, something we battle with our entire lives. It is therefore imperative that we communicate our feelings and emotions with our partner so that it gives an opportunity to meet somewhere in the middle and avoid unnecessary heartache. Gary Chapman said in his book, *The Five Love Languages,*

> "Encouragement requires empathy and seeing the world from your spouse's perspective. We must first learn what is important to our spouse. Only then can

we give encouragement. With verbal encouragement, we are trying to communicate, 'I know. I care. I am with you. How can I help?' We are trying to show that we believe in him and in his abilities. We are giving credit and praise."

SPEAK YOUR MIND

Communication is a very delicate matter and cannot be generalized easily. Every situation, every person, every culture interprets communication differently, and we must adapt to that in order to be good at it. I used to work for an airline in Asia where communication was a different animal than what I was used to in the United States. In the U.S., if a flight attendant noticed something happening in the back of the plane, he or she would immediately call us to tell us about it. In other cultures, that is not so much the case, often times having multiple barriers between the sources. For example, if something would happen in the back of the plane, the cabin crew would report this to their immediate supervisor working in the middle of the plane. That supervisor would then relay that information to their supervisor working up in first class. Then finally that person would call the flight deck and report the problem. Not only was potentially valuable time wasted, but the story can also change greatly when told to different people numerous times over. This is much like the game we play as young kids. We would all stand in a circle, and one person would whisper a short story in the next person's ear, then it was passed from person to person. When it circled around and came back to the first person who made up the story, almost every time the story was entirely different.

There was a Korean Airlines cargo jet that crashed in London back in 1999. The Captain had been talking to the First Officer in a very derogatory fashion prior to the crash. It seemed like every time the First Officer would speak, the Captain would somehow yell at him for something. So the communication channel was all but shut down. The plane took off and one of the primary flight instruments on the Captain's side failed. The First Officer, being afraid to speak since he had been getting yelled at all day, didn't directly inform the Captain of the situation that he correctly recognized. The instrument on his side was still working properly. Had he taken the controls, he would have been able to safely fly the airplane.

The Captain continued to follow his faulty instrument all the way to impact. The First Officer never really spoke up throughout the flight and was so afraid of speaking up or taking over the controls that he chose to die instead (with that being said, a lot of it had to do with their culture). In a marriage, you each set the tone for communication. If you bark back at your partner every time he or she tells you something, then chances are your partner will start to tell you less. Being able to listen is equally important as being able to speak. Therefore, make every effort to keep the communication channel open and welcomed not just at work but also at home with your family.

We must recognize our differences and adapt to them so that we can properly communicate with others, no matter what the circumstance may be. In a relationship, this is very much the same, as effective communication is crucial. I can't tell you how many times I have heard friends or colleagues complain about their spouses, but rarely have they brought up those complaints or concerns with them. The fear of conflict seems to be the most typical reason for this. Sometimes it's just easier to not say anything and move on, but is it really healthy? Of course, I am not saying to nag your partner about every little thing. There is also a lot to be said for "choosing your battles wisely."

"The single biggest problem in communication is the illusion that it has taken place."

George Bernard Shaw

CHAPTER 5
The Crazy Things We Do For Love

"The weak can never forgive.
Forgiveness is the attribute of the strong."

Mahatma Ghandi

We hear about people having affairs all the time; celebrities cheating on each other are almost on every cover of popular entertainment magazines. It's easy to blame one party or another for why an affair happened, but there has got to be more to it than "it's your own fault." Let's take Isaac Newton's famous physics law, "For every action there is an opposite and equal reaction," and reverse-engineer it. The reaction (the affair) is a result of an action (the relationship or something occurring within). So instead of assigning blame to others, you have to take a look in the mirror first. If your spouse cheated on you, ask yourself what you have done to cause them to do it in the first place.

Herein lies one of the greatest challenges we face in our profession. We don't like to take this approach because doing so is admitting and recognizing our own faults and imperfections. Of course there are always exceptions, but it is rare that a guy has a cheating spouse and has done nothing at all to cause an affair. If nothing else, your being gone half of the month flying, wouldn't that alone be a reason? The reason is often times something completely unintentional but nonetheless consequential. You have to look at all the factors involved. Some you can control; yet, some you cannot, but recognizing the imperfections will help determine the root cause and allow opportunity to mitigate the damages. Only after the underlying causes are identified can real change take place. Otherwise, the same issues typically will arise again.

Then comes the issue of forgiveness. Is that something possible or not after a certain event? Love is an incredible power that causes us to not only do the most unimaginable things in life, but that also allows us the ability to forgive. Reinhold Niebuhr said, "Forgiveness is the final form of love."

All the things we do for love. Think about how many wars have been fought, lives lost, and empires destroyed all in the name of love. This next story is almost unbelievable, but it actually happened. It is a story about determination and forgiveness. I asked Steve to help me with it, so I made sure I didn't miss anything.

Breaking Rambo's Heart

Steve was raised by a Cuban family in Miami. He worked hard to have the things that he did. His father was a successful businessman in Cuba, until one day he was falsely accused of hiding money and was imprisoned for five years. Steve's mother raised the family alone until they were reunited with their dad and moved to the United States. Five years in prison was enough for his father to have a whole new outlook on life, and he did his best to pass this down to his children. He believed in not taking things for granted and always giving your best at what you set out to do. Never give up hope, no matter how grim the situation.

Steve loved aviation and always wanted to fly airplanes for a living. He also loved his country for giving him and his family such amazing opportunities. So he decided to enlist in the Marine Corps during the first Iraq invasion. Today, he is known among his colleagues at work for his love and passion of the martial arts. I have personally known him for years and remember the days when we were killing time in the crashpad, Steve would practice moves on us that he said were always one step away from death. He would noodle us around, and the next thing you knew, you'd be twisted up like a pretzel, barely able to breathe, and then he would explain how easy it would be to end your life in that that position. I'm glad we were of great use to him for practice, but more importantly he would train for hours and hours at the gym. He would bounce around the crash pad like a rabid kangaroo, pushing furniture around and pulling himself up on the door frames. He was determined and dedicated to accomplish his goals. No one would stand in the way of that.

When Steve returned from the war, he wanted to pursue his dreams of becoming a pilot and started to look at flight schools. The cost was astronomical, and having just been overseas, he didn't save a lot of money. During this time he also met his soon-to-be fiancé and they moved into a small apartment together. She always had dreamt of becoming a nurse and was interviewing at numerous schools in the Miami area. While doing research for flight schools, Steve discovered that the Coast Guard was looking to accept candidates for flight slots. They would cover the expenses of flight training and then he could fly out of South Florida once qualified. What a great opportunity; this could be his golden ticket he thought. During this time, his fiancé also found a perfect nursing program; but unlike Steve's free ride, she would have to take on big loans to pay for the program. The problem with her plan was that she would not be able to work at all during her schooling. So if Steve went to the Coast Guard training, they would not have enough money to pay the bills. It was decision time. One of them would have to put their dreams on hold; the other would pursue them.

Steve has always been a loving, caring, and kind person, so it didn't surprise me to hear that he gave in and let his fiancé begin her nursing program. He took a small loan out to get his flight instructor ratings, then worked at a local flight school and waited tables at night to pay their bills. For him this was a huge setback in his career path. Instead of going to free flight school and then having a nice, secure flying job in the Coast Guard, he was teaching people how not to kill themselves doing touch and go's at their local airport. She was happier than ever because her dreams of becoming a nurse were becoming a reality and she couldn't wait to begin.

A few months later, Steve made some good contacts at the airport where he was instructing. One individual he met had a small charter company. He liked Steve and saw how motivated he was, so he offered him a job in the right seat of an old Learjet. Steve was excited to get this offer and gladly accepted. Before he knew it, he was flying all over the country and building valuable flight time. Now that he had a good job and felt more secure financially, the two decided to get married and move into a small house near her nursing school. Things were going well; the thought of having passed up an incredible opportunity in the Coast Guard was overcome by bliss and love, both for his new wife and his new job flying a fast jet around the country. His wife finished training at the top of her class and found a nice job at a nearby hospital. All was well in his world. What could possibly go wrong?

One evening after dinner, Steve was cleaning up in the kitchen when he overheard his wife in the other room talking rather quietly into the phone. He thought it was rather strange but didn't think much more of it. A few days later he found himself in a similar situation but this time decided to take action. After she hung up the phone, and while she was getting ready for bed, he snuck in the other room and dialed *69 (these were the days before caller ID) and called the number it gave him. He was very surprised to hear that it was a doctor who he knew worked with his wife. Shocked and confused, he quickly hung up the phone and went to bed. He didn't know what to say to his wife, but began to question things as suddenly his world started to fill with doubt.

Keep in mind, Steve was a person with incredible determination and motivation, he was a marine and true warrior. He would get to the bottom of this no matter what.

No one would mess with his life. So a few days later, Steve snuck in the other room, paged himself on his company beeper, and called a friend who was pretending to be the company dispatch. He acted angry and upset as he repeated back all the cities he would have to fly to, making sure she could hear his reaction, a trip that would certainly keep him out for a few days. He hung up the phone, went to his wife in the other room, and told her he had to leave right away. He packed his suitcase, but this time, he secretly tossed in all his climbing gear he owned and then placed his clothes on top to hide any evidence. He kissed his wife good-bye and headed to the airport, so she thought. He drove to his friends' house and began to finalize his plans for the next day.

Could this really be happening to him, could his loving wife be having an affair? He knew a few guys in his unit that came home to discover their wives had moved on and started new lives with other men who were around more often. Could the schedule at his corporate job be keeping him out too long? After all, she was the reason why he was working there anyway, if it wasn't for her, he would have joined the Coast Guard and would flying at a cushy job right now. He decided to sleep on it and would decide the next day how to proceed. He tossed and turned most of the night trying desperately to get a few hours of sleep, but no luck. He was on an emotional roller coaster. On one extreme, he felt angry that she might be cheating on him; on the other extreme, he felt ashamed that he would even think she would do that to him.

D-DAY

The sun came up and shined brightly through the gap in the curtains; it was decision time. He took a quick shower, poured a cup of coffee, and then made up his mind. He had to find out for certain if she was having an affair or not, period. He thanked his friend for the hospitality and drove his car toward the hospital where he knew his wife would be working all day, the same hospital as the guy she was secretly talking to the other night. He parked the car a few blocks from the hospital and then walked to the front entrance carrying his little duffel bag that he strategically packed the night before. He walked up to the front entrance sliding doors but recognized the ladies working behind the information desk. They had seen him many times bringing his wife lunch or coffee in the past. He patiently waited until someone walked through the doors and asked for help, figuring that would surely distract the ladies. Steve took this opportunity to sneak in and walk past the ladies that certainly would have recognized him if it wasn't for his wearing a baseball hat and their distraction of helping the person who just walked in ahead of Steve.

He proceeded down a long hallway and walked into the men's restroom. He locked himself in one of the stalls and opened his duffel bag. Inside, there was a camouflage jacket and pants, lots of climbing rope, numerous carabiners, and camouflage face paint. When he was done changing, he basically looked identical to Rambo. He was just locked in a hospital restroom instead of war-torn Burma. He packed his old clothes in the bag, took a peek under the stalls to make sure the restroom was still empty, and proceeded to the door. He barely opened it and made sure no one was coming down the hallway. It was clear, so Steve hustled down the long hallway toward the big atrium.

The atrium was beautiful inside and had lots of big trees under which picnic tables were set up for the hospital staff to eat lunch. It was still early, so the atrium was empty, making a clear path to the tallest tree located in the center of it. Steve walked up to the base of the huge tree, threw a long rope up to the nearest branch, and up he went. He climbed to the highest branch, secured himself with the ropes and carabiners, and waited. It didn't take long for him to start second-guessing himself. What in the world was he doing up in that tree, he thought. He was painted up and decked out like Rambo, harnessed way up in a tree located inside a hospital.

What if someone saw him, what if the police were called, how would he explain his criminal record during an interview at an airline one day? Right then the first few hospital staff walked into the atrium carrying food trays. They sat all around at the picnic tables and enjoyed the peace and quiet the atrium offered. Steve got out his binoculars and searched for his wife, no luck. People came, ate, left, and more people would come in. The place became very busy, and he started to wonder if his wife would ever arrive. What if this whole production was for nothing, a complete waste of time?

Lunch hour passed, and there was still no sign of his wife. He then started thinking of an exit plan. But right about that time, another two staff members walked into the atrium, arm in arm, carrying a single tray of food. They walked right up to the giant tree Steve was in, sat at the picnic table at its base, and proceeded to have a lovely romantic lunch. Steve almost fell out of the tree when he realized that the two people were actually his wife and this mysterious doctor he heard on the phone. He didn't know whether to be angry and disappointed or happy because his plan succeeded. He was right. His hunch was correct, and his crazy plan had actually worked. But now what, how could he prove that he knew, and now how should he confront them? The two below finished lunch and while Steve was contemplating what his next move should be, the two start kissing and became more and more indulged in each other, since they were now the only two in the atrium, or so they thought. This was just too much for Steve to handle. He couldn't just sit there and watch.

He started to untie all his ropes and harnesses, almost falling out of the tree a few times because of his shaky hands. All free, he secured a rope down the tree and repelled down to the ground. The two were too preoccupied by each other, failing to notice Rambo appearing out of the tree and standing a few feet next to where they were sitting. He again had no idea what his next move would be, as he was rather surprised that they didn't notice him yet. He figured since the doctor relied on his hands for work, he would simply breaks his wrists and that would teach him a good lesson. But then he started to think about the consequences, and luckily, talked himself out of that plan. He took a few steps forward, reached his hand out, and tapped the doctor firmly on the shoulder. The doctor turned around, saw the Rambo lookalike and froze.

Steve later told me that he has heard of people turning white but never actually saw it happen, until that day. After a few seconds of just pure shock, the doctor let go of Steve's wife's hands and ran out of the atrium. Steve's wife stood there completely in shock and almost couldn't even recognize her husband behind all the face paint and the camouflage outfit. Steve looked at her and said simply, "I can't believe you would do this to me," then walked away calmly.

He remembers hearing her shout a few things at him like, "It's not what it looks like," or "Let me explain," but he just kept walking. Straight down the hall, around the corner and right toward the information desk he snuck by a few hours earlier. Right then he saw a security officer walking briskly toward him. He figured the doctor must have called security, but at that point he was so angry that he really didn't care and just kept walking. As the officer got closer, he saw the Rambo look alike, gave him a confused look, and turned around. Thinking back to that moment, if you saw a guy walking down a hospital hallway dressed like Rambo, you couldn't blame the officer for being a little scared and intimidated. Steve walked right by the ladies behind the desk, wished them a good day, and headed outside toward his car. Can you imagine what those nice ladies behind the desk must have thought about the moment they saw Rambo wish them a "nice day?" Steve went back to his friends' house and now faced the realities of what had just happened.

How Can I Ever Trust You Again?

Bernard Meltzer once said, "When you forgive, you in no way change the past - but you sure do change the future." Steve's heart was crushed; he was deeply hurt. He had given up his flying opportunity of a lifetime just for her, and this is how his wife repaid him? But he also knew that being angry and hateful toward her would accomplish nothing and certainly not change what happened. This was the crossroad where Steve had to make a decision as to which path to travel down. One was to separate and move on with his life without her. The other was to try to determine why the situation happened in the first place and see if there was any possibility of repairing the damage. Proverbs 10:12, "Hatred stirs up dissension, but love covers over all wrongs."

Steve decided to give love and forgiveness a try. His wife apologized for days, and they made appointments with a marriage counselor. This healing process went on for a few months but the wounds were too deep, and Steve knew deep down in his heart that he would never be able to trust her again. He knew he would pursue his dreams of flying, which meant that any relationship that he might make work would solely rely on trust, something he would never have with his wife again. He loved her enough to let her go, not for what she had done but for what she would not be able to offer him in the future, trust. Steve filed for a divorce, and thereby, their love story ended.

In this profession trust is a crucial element. Without it,

the probability that it will sustain the periods of absence is slim to none. "Trusting another after having your heart broken is very hard. But you have to remember the relationship is nothing without trust. Don't bring bricks from your old relationship, you'll build the same house." - Unknown Author

Don't worry, Steve found his happy ending after all. He met his future second wife a few years later, fathered two beautiful children and they are living happily ever after so far. It took Steve years to be able to tell this story and laugh about how crazy it sounds when you really think about it. His dressing up like Rambo could have ended in so many different ways that day in the tree. It's almost comical to think of many of them. Besides the comical aspect here in Steve's story, there is much more to it than a good laugh.

What does this story say about Steve's determination? He set out on a mission and accomplished it, at all costs. This is the type of personality that each one of us possesses inside; some people just haven't been put in a situation that has called upon us to need to display such attributes. Think of all the obstacles laid out before each of us to become a professional pilot. How many chances are there to fail? Even once you land your dream job, you still have to prove yourself every six to 12 months, and ultimately, your job depends on it. In the end, Steve chose to forgive his wife and even though they may not have made it work in the long run, he still forgave her.

Forgiving his wife was Steve's first crucial step in moving on with his life, a step that led to finding true love later on in his life. Too many people we fly with are hateful and hold grudges against their ex partners. Then they go on and meet a new spouse, get married, and are surprised that the new marriage ends the same as the first one. A recent article on the Psychology Today website said, "Past statistics have shown that in the U.S. 50 percent of first marriages, 67 percent of second, and 73 percent of third marriages end in divorce." These numbers are for regular couples, not ones in the transportation industry, which is much higher. Why is that you think? There are almost always causes that you are solely responsible for, which played a vital role in a divorce. You have to be honest with yourself and face those causes in order to ensure that they will not play a part in your next relationship. The people who are hard headed, and ignore such causes, oftentimes end up in the same situation, different spouse. The people who truly and honestly learn from their past and make the necessary changes, are usually the ones who have their "happily ever after."

Steve chose to learn from his relationship, determine the causes of why things went south, and made the necessary changes in his own life to ensure they wouldn't happen again. The most important part of this is to know and respect your own limitations. Steve knew that he would never be able to fully trust his wife again. In this job, trust is like the root to a plant. The root provides nutrition to grow and thrive, and support and strength for when storms roar overhead. Without it, our relationships will not endure the challenges and difficult times we spend apart from loved ones during our careers. Steve gave up his dreams for his wife to go to nursing school. She then betrayed him by having an affair with a coworker, leaving Steve crushed and broken. But instead of him continuing to be angry and hateful, he started to think about what may have caused her to betray him in the first place. As Nelson Mandela said, "Resentment is like drinking poison and then hoping it will kill your enemies," With that in mind, Steve let go of resentment and moved forward with is life. He knew that he would need to find a spouse who would be able to handle his schedules, with trust as the foundation of their relationship, and he did just that.

It's rare that you find a couple, happily married, and suddenly one has an affair out of the blue. When you begin to analyze their circumstances, you almost always quickly discover that the process that led to the affair began a long time ago. When you can identify these signs, which eventually begin to crumble a relationship, you will recognize them when they come up and will be able to mitigate them. It's much easier to fight an enemy that you can see than one that is hidden among you.

CHAPTER 6
Your Mind Is Playing Tricks on You

"The conscious mind may be compared to a fountain playing in the sun and falling back into the great subterranean pool of subconscious from which is rises."

Sigmund Freud

When we first meet our spouse, we are overcome by excitement and passion. People always say that the flame burns down after a few months. Well this is true for the most part. Your conscious mind is completely blind to the realities that sometimes lie behind the phase of "new love." Think about someone you know or have met that you really didn't like and thought they were just the meanest, most selfish person in the world. You couldn't imagine spending five minutes with them and certainly not a lifetime. For every one of those, there is another person who thinks the complete opposite and can't imagine a life without that person. How many friends do you know that have dated or even married someone you thought was a terrible choice? How can you see something so clearly about someone that they simply cannot? How many times did your parents tell you to either do something or not do something that you disagreed with 100 percent? Then later in life, you realize that they were right all along, you just didn't realize it at that time. Well this is where we get into the conscious and subconscious mind dilemma.

Before I continue with this chapter, please know that this is only my observation over the years working with hundreds of others and also observing different cultures around the world. These are also only observations in heterosexual relationships. Some might take offense or flat out disagree. But again, this is only my observation so please don't take it personally. I wasn't sure if I would even include this chapter in this book but ended up deciding that I might as well, so here you go.

SURVIVAL OF THE FITTEST

Let's look at a relationship from the basic elements. I want to detach from judgment for a moment and look at things from a "nature" and "genetic" aspect. A man, generally speaking, is at first attracted to a woman whom he finds very attractive. Typically, when looking for a spouse, you don't approach a woman, who you find absolutely unattractive, to see if she has a nice personality. Not to be mean, but that's just the way it is for the most part. So now you meet an attractive woman, and you two hit it off and begin a romantic relationship. Now the battle between the minds begins.

On a conscious level, you are attracted to this person physically, ignoring all other characteristics that may not be so positive. At the same time your subconscious, the behind the scenes machine, is looking to reproduce. I know this sounds impersonal to many of you, but that's the way it is. It's natural, and it's what you think about, whether you know it or not. Your subconscious is looking at making a strong offspring, children who will be smart in society, strong to reach the top, and good looking enough to find a worthy mate and reproduce again to carry on your genes. So you look for qualities that will compensate for ones you might be lacking or be missing. Ever wonder why you see stunningly beautiful women married to average-looking a guys? How many couples do you know where it's the opposite?

Let's look at the other end of the equation. Women seek men who are obviously attractive, but more importantly, who are able to provide. The ability for a man to provide makes him more attractive to her, and so this helps explain why you often see a really good-looking woman with a so-so looking man, if he is able to provide well. The woman wants to feel secure, ensuring that shelter and food is provided for her offspring. So the guy is attracted to her because she will produce good offspring, she is attracted to him because he will provide protection, shelter, and/or a stable home and environment to raise her offspring and be safe. Sounds like a pretty good arrangement wouldn't you say? This same concept applies to most animals as well; funny how that works in nature, isn't it? Ever heard of "Survival of the Fittest?" M. Scott Peck wrote in *The Road Less Traveled*,

"Falling in love is not an act of will. It is not a conscious choice. No matter how open to or eager for it we may be, the experience may still elude us. Contrarily, the experience may capture us at times when we are definitely not seeking it, when it is inconvenient and undesirable. We are as likely to fall in love with someone with whom we are obviously ill matched as with someone more suitable. Indeed, we may not even like or admire the object of our passion, yet, try as we might, we may not be able to fall in love with a person whom we deeply respect and with whom a deep relationship would be in all ways desirable. This is not to say that the experience of falling in love is immune to discipline . . . We can choose how to respond to the experience of falling in love, but we cannot choose the experience itself"

BEAUTY AND THE BEAST

Let's make up an example to illustrate this and see if it sounds like something you have seen or heard in real life. Marc is a banker at a national bank and is in his late twenties. A lot of college meant just as much drinking and not taking care of himself, so he is carrying around a little extra weight. He also had bad acne in high school, and his face still shows the scars from those years. He is a loving and kind person, has lots of good friendships, and is set in a career to be very successful. Kat on the other hand is a mid-twenties college dropout, works at a fashion-clothing store in the mall, and models part time for local newspapers and ads. She never stays in relationships for more than a few months and is known to have a mean streak. She has new friends all the time and wonders why they never seem to stick around long. She lives in a small two-bedroom apartment, which she shares with a high school friend, still driving her car that she bought for a few hundred dollars during her senior year in high school.

One Friday after work, Marc and some friends go to a local Irish bar to celebrate one of their birthdays. He walks up to the bar and accidentally bumps into Kat and spills her beer. He apologizes, and while waiting for her new beer to arrive, they begin chatting. Initially, Marc finds her very attractive and can't even believe she is giving him the time of the day. Kat is open to talking to Marc, notices his nice suit, and enjoys their conversation. Long story short, the two exchange numbers and begin dating after a few phone calls and text messages back and forth. Marc's friends are happy for him but notice her mean streak. It was so obvious to them that they started to tease him by saying that she was wearing the pants in the relationship and so forth. Marc ignores their concerns, and after another few months go by, they get engaged and marry a year later. Gary Chapman said in his book, *The Five Love Languages*, "The person who is 'in-love' has the illusion that his beloved is perfect."

Marc and Kat buy a nice house together, two new cars, and the next thing you know, baby number one is born, followed shortly after by baby number two. Their relationship is average. He is stressed at work and works long hours, she is even more stressed raising the two kids and taking care of the household. Marc and Kat fight mostly about money and about things like raising the kids, issues that are very typical in marriage. Kat spends money freely, and Marc is frustrated to see that his paychecks disappear almost instantly. Marc enjoys hanging out with his buddies from work and spends most Saturdays playing golf with his buddies. Kat also enjoys spending time with her girlfriends at the beauty salons and spa. The key to this is that they both enjoy things that do not involve the other. Of course, we all need our own time, but we also need to spend time doing things with our spouses that we both enjoy.

Fast forward, and after 18 years of this lifestyle, the kids go off to college, and now it's time for Marc and Kat to be alone again after all this time. She has always wanted to travel and felt like now was a perfect time to do this. Marc enjoyed playing golf with his buddies on the weekend and would rather not travel with his wife. After all, she was always yelling at him, and he really didn't like spending time with her. Kat and her friends decide to go out and take a few week-long trips. Along the way, they meet other men who have similar interests. She comes home and yells at her husband, why he couldn't be more like them. Tired of getting yelled at, Marc would phone his buddies and meet up with them at the Irish bar where he first met his wife. The scene was lively, and he started chatting with younger women that were hanging out there. Of course, the heavy job of raising two kids took a toll on his wife's physical appearance, and her aging was starting to show. Kat wants Marc to be more like the guys she met while traveling; Marc wants Kat to look more like the younger girls he meets at the bar.

Long story short, next thing you know they get divorced. Kat spends her days traveling with friends and enjoying having enough income from the divorce to not have to work anytime soon. She is still very attractive and soon meets a new man, slightly older than she is, and also previously married with kids. They marry shortly after meeting, and she once again find herself in a very comfortable life. Marc meets a younger woman at the bar and loves the fact that he is dating someone the same age as his wife when he first met her. His friends immediately see the same personality in Marc's new girlfriend as his wife displayed back then, but Marc again ignores their concerns, blinded by his subconscious mind to mate. After a few short months they also get married, and now Marc's new wife wants to have kids with him.

Voila! There you have it, the entire circle is complete, and on it's way to make another full circle. Marc's conscious and subconscious have tricked him again, and he is right back where he was years prior when meeting his first wife, just to end up the same as before again. As Augustus of Rome said, "If we could survive without a wife, citizens of Rome, all of us would do without that nuisance; but since nature has so decreed that we cannot manage comfortably with them, nor live in any way without them, we must plan for our lasting preservation rather than for our temporary pleasure".

WHAT ARE YOU BRINGING TO THE TABLE?

Let's examine Marc and Kat for a moment. Marc was initially attracted to Kat because of her looks. The fact that she was mean and never kept the same friends for long didn't matter, even after he got to know her better. He was thinking offspring. Even after he learned about her negative qualities, his conscious told him that she might be offering a lifetime of misery, but his subconscious overshadowed those thoughts. Kat, on the other hand, was thinking that Marc was giving her all the attention she wanted. He had a great job and could certainly provide for her and any possible children to come. Her boyfriends in the past were really good looking and younger than her, but all ended badly because they were too immature. So Marc was in it for Kat's physical appearance, and Kat was in it for Marc's ability to provide. She brings to the relationship her ability to raise two beautiful kids; he provides a nice safe house with food on the table.

They raise their kids, basically become roommates along the way, and then once the kids are out of the house, the subconscious releases the conscious mind. Now the reality sets in; Marc realizes that he doesn't really like Kat that much, but she did raise his children. Kat realizes that Marc provided for her to be able to raise the kids, but now she doesn't like him that much either. The only bond and common interest that kept them together for all this time was now out of the house.

Marc is back at the bar. When he meets younger women, his subconscious mind once again takes over all reason, and he wants to start the process over again. Once again, he is attracted to women who almost certainly will promise a lifetime of misery and unhappiness, but once again, his conscious is overcome by other thoughts. Kat has raised her kids, and knowing that she is now past her childbearing age, she wants to go out and do the things she has always wanted.

So she travels with her girlfriends and meets men who have similar interests, falls in love with one easily since she really didn't love Marc anymore, and she starts her new life.

Ever hear women complain about the older guys trying to hit on them at bars? Why do you think they are hitting on them and not so much women closer to them in age? It is very common to find the man older than the woman, but you rarely find a man much younger than the woman in the relationship. "Someone told me the delightful story of the crusader who put a chastity belt on his wife and gave the key to his best friend for safekeeping, in case of his death. He had ridden only a few miles away when his friend, riding hard, caught up with him, saying 'You gave me the wrong key,'" said Anais Nin.

LOVE FOR THE RIGHT REASONS

Say what you want, but I am willing to bet that you know someone in your life that has gone through this same exact cycle. I know it sounds harsh and insensitive, but luckily, it is oftentimes is not this way, and people actually love each other not for what they can offer, but for who they are. The key element is to pick your partner wisely, and even more importantly for the right reasons. If you can somehow manage to avoid having your subconscious overshadow your conscious, you might be able to make the right decision in picking a partner that you can grow old with and share your happily ever after together.

In our jobs, we are required to be gone a good part of the

month, so keep in mind that whomever you end up with needs to be independent and able to run things while you are away. Trust is also vital to any relationship that is to endure our careers. So if your relationship begins out of an affair, difficult times will lie ahead. Think of it like this, if you meet someone who is in another relationship and you end up together, what is to prevent them from doing the same again in the future? It takes a certain kind of person to come home at night and be able to lie to their partner. If they can pull it off once, then why not again later to you? We are all different, and luckily, there is someone for everyone. You just have to trust that you will find them.

"TAKE 2"

You would think that the second marriage would have a higher success rate than the first, but that is very wrong indeed. If we take a check ride and fail an engine failure maneuver, you practice that maneuver over and over and then retake the test. Usually by then you have mastered the skill and pass the second check ride with flying colors. However, would you want to travel in an airplane with a pilot up front who has failed an engine failure maneuver multiple times over and over? Bottom-line, we learn from previous mistakes, make the necessary adjustments and then perfect the maneuver. So why is it that we can do this in our jobs but fail to do so in our own personal lives? You would think that if someone was married before and it didn't work out, they would choose a better partner and not make the same mistakes over again.

There are numerous schools of thought for this concept, and I want to share a few of them now. There are those people who meet someone when they are both truly single, and then there are those who overlap relationships.

MORALS

I have met several people who met their second or third wife while married; rarely do those marriages last. To be able to be in a committed relationship and yet meet someone else, you have to have a certain level of moral detachment. The fact that you were able to go home to your wife even though you are involved with someone else says something about your ability to lie and mislead. Your "secret partner," the cheating partner, also has to possess a level of moral right and wrong. That partner knows that what is going on is wrong yet continues to do so. So if you have it in you to do it once, then why not do it again in the future?

We already discussed how important trust is in our line of profession, and eventually that comes back to haunt the second or third marriages that started this way. Something will happen that triggers doubt. That's when the road to divorce begins again, since you start to wonder if the very same thing that led to your relationship in the first place is now starting again, just with someone else. For the spouse at home, they will also always wonder if you are involved with someone else, just like the way they met you in the first place. Being married obviously did not stop you or them before, so why should it now?

To make matters worse, the momentary reward of the new

relationship actually encourages this type of behavior. For example, if a married guy meets a new woman and leaves his wife for her, then he was rewarded for his behavior with a new relationship. I call this a momentary reward, because it too will die off just like the previous marriage. A relationship that begins in a bed of lies and sneaking around will usually lead to the same bed with just a different partner lying next to you. Would you deposit money with a company that was previously shut down for cheating customers out of money, but then re-emerged as a new company under a new name? Would your decision be different if all the executives and managers were new ones?

TIME IS A HEALER

It is not until the individual truly realizes and accepts their part in a failed marriage that change can occur. When this change occurs, things that went wrong the first time around likely will not happen again. This process takes time and a lot of soul searching, something that comes naturally with time. Ever wonder why people tell you not to be a rebound in a new relationship? You cannot realize all the things that went wrong in a relationship and then fix them overnight. With that being said, we are also subject to what our jobs require of us. Usually, that means a lot of time away from home. If your first marriage did not work out because you were gone too much, then it might be a good idea to pick a partner who can handle such a schedule.

Marriages that start while you are already in this career usually have a higher success rate than those that started before that type of lifestyle. Many military couples do very well in aviation, simply because they are used to longer periods of time apart from their spouses. For many in fact, a two-week trip is a cakewalk compared to 60 days away on deployments. Couples who meet in college face a more difficult challenge where after college one of them goes off to become a pilot. They are used to one lifestyle and see each other often. Then suddenly, one is gone half of the month. Some are able to adapt and do great; others, not so much. You must recognize your capability in what you are willing to deal with in a relationship, and then you must stay true to those limitations. Only then can you give a relationship your fullest try because you are not only staying within what you can handle, but also staying true to yourself.

"Let us not seek to fix the blame for the past, let us accept our own responsibility for the future."

John F. Kennedy

CHAPTER 7
Temptations

"We accept the love we think we deserve."
Stephen Chbosky

Why is the divorce rate so much higher for us in the traveling industry than it is for the regular crowd? Is it because we are gone from home for too long? How about the cheating factor? Do our relationships suffer from more divorces as a result of affairs and unfaithfulness? If so, is it the fact that we are away from home and that there is more opportunity to cheat? Or could it be our personalities that lead us into temptations? The reality is that we are all subject to temptations. No matter what line of work you are in, it's how you handle the temptations that makes a difference.

How do you handle temptations? I have a good friend who flies for one of the world's largest airlines based in Dubai. He is single and absolutely loves his job. He flies to the most exotic and interesting cities all around the world, and to top that off is surrounded by gorgeous, young, and fun flight attendants. They spend days away from Dubai and explore the cities together while on overnights, often times late dinners and sometimes even just him and a female colleague. He is a single guy. The nights are innocent and it's just that. But what if he had a wife at home while he was out on a trip having dinner with a female colleague, how do you think she would feel about that?

Are You Lonely Tonight?

That is one of the greatest challenges while on overnights away from home. We spend half of our lives with people other than our spouses, often for weeks on end. My buddy, for example, might go on a 10-day trip around the world with the other pilot and 20 flight attendants. Is he supposed to go explore all the sights on his own and eat dinners alone? It is much easier to pass time when you are with other people, especially since they are going through the same things that you are with being gone from home. I know my friend has made lots of new friendships on the road. He figures that if you are going to be gone from home anyway, you might as well enjoy your time. This may sound very simple for us on the road, but we are the ones who are out and about. The spouse that stays behind, on the other hand, experiences something entirely different. They are home taking care of things, often raising children alone. While we may be out running around exotic destinations with members of the opposite sex, they are stuck back at home.

While in Dubai I met Dave, one of my friend's training partners from when they were initially hired. He left his previous life behind and moved his wife and three children over to Dubai. It's a whole new world for all of them, new surroundings, new culture, and new friends. While Dave goes out on an eight-day trip with 20 beautiful flight attendants, his wife is left at home taking care of the new home and the family.

So when he calls at night to check in with them, should he tell her about galloping around Paris with his crew? But at the same time, should he not mention it and risk being accused of not sharing his life with her? Would she be upset knowing that he was out with other women? Shouldn't she be happy for him and trust him? It doesn't take a genius to figure out when a good time is to share stories with your spouse. We must each individually decide what to share and when the best timing is. The important thing is to keep in mind the perspective of the other spouse and respect the circumstances they are in, as well your own.

Innocent But Looking Guilty

I remember a time where the Captain, Joe, and myself were at a restaurant and bar overseas. While we were having a nice conversation we saw two women sitting at a bench style table across the room. They were trying to tell this older gentleman, who clearly had too much to drink, to take a hike. He wouldn't leave them alone so we finally decided to step in and help. We walked over and sat with them, acting like we belonged to the table, which quickly got the drunk man to leave. They were thankful, and we started a conversation with them. They were from the same hometown as Joe, so they naturally had a lot in common. Since they were visiting the city we were in, they had their cameras out and wanted us to take a few pictures of them. Joe happened to be in one of them but we didn't really think much more of it. We finished our drinks, wished them a nice vacation, and went our merry ways.

The next morning I got a panicked call from Joe. He had received a friend request from a social media site, remembering that they had a picture of him. He shared the account with his wife; if she saw that picture she would lose it. Here her husband is away in a foreign land, and then there is a picture of him with two other women at a restaurant/bar. This goes to show you how easily an innocent situation can lead to a really big issue, even though it was truly harmless. This is where trust and respect is truly tested. Had his wife seen the picture, surely she would have trusted that nothing happened between Joe and the two girls in the photo, but is it respectful for him to be in the photo in the first place? It's a fine line, one that must be walked down carefully. Something may appear innocent, but put yourself in the other persons shoes to see how a situation might be perceived. The moral of the story is to consider the outcome of your actions, even though they might seem innocent at the time, they might not look so innocent to your spouse at home.

NEW FRIENDS, AND MORE

Brad was in initial training overseas for an international airline. He lived in Chicago and had a nice home where he and his wife of 20 years lived, childless. Training was to last six months, the longest they had ever been apart. Their marriage was good, and they got along just fine. Brad said he felt comfortable and secure in his marriage, but that was it. The fire was gone, a small flame burning, at best. They had become roommates, good friends that lived together under the same roof. Their romantic life consisted of a casual good night kiss, the occasional bed romance, but nothing as far passionate love. He had flown for a corporate flight department at home, was gone on average 10 days a month, and enjoyed playing golf with his coworkers. She was a teacher at the local middle school and coached the girls' volleyball team. Life was fine. It was comfortable and always remained in the comfort zone. Suddenly he found himself in a foreign exotic land where he knew no one except his fellow classmates.

Training was stressful and required a lot of late nights up studying. On days off, many of his fellow trainees would go to the downtown area and enjoy nice restaurants and a vibrant nightlife. Most would go back to their hotel fairly early to rest for the next day in training, but Brad would often stay out a little longer and started to make some local friends. Next thing you know, he was not only going out more often, but also was hanging out with his new friends and subsequently, their friends. One night, at a nice restaurant with a group of people, he met a local woman. She was in her mid thirties, eight years younger than him and was stunningly beautiful. Her dark hair and darker skin enchanted Brad and he couldn't take his eyes off her. The dinner came to an end, and Brad went back to his hotel. The woman he had just met was all he could think about; he had a difficult time focusing on his training.

A few days passed and he was once again invited to a nice dinner party. He went, and wouldn't you have guessed it, she was there again. This time Brad was determined to talk to her more and get to know her. They had a lot in common, as she ran a successful business herself and shared many of the same interests as Brad did. They exchanged numbers and began going out all the time. She would sit with him while he was studying, she would quiz him while walking on the beach, and what was at first a friendship quickly developed into a romantic relationship. Brad was totally in love. For the first time in more than 20 years he had feelings he forgot existed. Sure he loved his wife back home, but he was "in love" with this woman.

Time flew by, and before he knew it, he had finished training and was to go home again. Brad now found himself at a crossroad, what should he do? He knew he should break up with his new love and try to fix his marriage back home, but he couldn't imagine breaking things off with his girlfriend. He later said that he felt like being at dinner with his family as a young teenager, newly in love. Of course you loved your parents and siblings, but you really wanted to finish dinner so you could call your girlfriend. At the time, you couldn't imagine loving anyone else, counting down the seconds before you could hear her voice. If your parents told you that this girlfriend was no good for you, you would have told them to get lost, they surely didn't understand. That's how he felt. He knew what he was doing was wrong; all of his peers told him so every day. But he simply didn't listen, didn't care, and thought no one really understood. The "new love" feelings blinded him from seeing clearly, something that we all have felt at one point or another in our lives. Think back to something you really pursued, just to look back later and wonder what on earth you were thinking. It could be a relationship, car, house, or just something little like eating at a shady restaurant because you were so hungry.

I'm a Victim

Anyway, he flew back home and was immediately right back to same old grind as he was before he left for initial training. He was at home and back to his usual life, roommates with his wife, and the days passed by as usual. He would go on his trips, and most would layover in the same city where his girlfriend lived. He lived for work, only here did he truly feel alive and in love. When he was home, he felt numb, going through the motions of the daily routine, but thinking constantly of when he could go back to work. This went on for a few months until the guilt started to eat at him. His peers continued to tell him that he needed to face the reality of his situation, but again, he felt like he was actually a victim of love. Feeling like a victim may have made the situation easier for Brad to cope with, as he convinced himself he was not at fault. He "loved" one woman and at the same time was "in love" with another, something that just happened and that he had no control over, so he thought. On one hand, he didn't want to hurt his wife and leave her, after all they spent over half of their lives together. On the other, he didn't want break up with his girlfriend, with whom he was so in love.

After much thought and deliberation, Brad decided to leave his wife, give her all of their belongings since he felt so bad, and move to the foreign city where he could be with his girlfriend. Brad and his girlfriend moved in together, got engaged a few months later, then married soon after that. They truly are happy and remain madly in love even at the time of this writing. His wife was not as upset as he thought she would be. She moved on and also is living her own happily ever after. They even remained friends and wished each other well on the holidays and birthdays. Over time, they both realized that they were living as roommates under the same roof, but both were too scared to face the reality of the situation. They had become close friends, but had no romantic connection. Holding on to their friendship at least made it seem like the years together gave them good memories and an everlasting bond they would always cherish. As Lauren Oliver says, "I guess that's just part of loving people: You have to give things up. Sometimes you even have to give them up."

Could they have tried to reignite their love? What if Brad had not stayed out later than his classmates and not made those new friends? By no means am I saying that Brad acted responsibly and was right, but in the end it worked out for him. The moral of the story is that you cannot avoid temptation, but often times you can avoid tempting situations. Don't put yourself in situations that might lead to temptation in the first place; that's much simpler. You have to know yourself and your limitations, know how you handle temptation, and if you're weak, then avoid it altogether.

TEMPTING SITUATIONS

Brad, for instance, had been gone from home for months

at a time during training. He was married but not romantically connected to his wife. He, therefore, was extremely vulnerable meeting someone else when the opportunity arose. With that said, he could have avoided situations that had the potential to lead to him meeting another woman. Of course, not all situations allow you to control this; but in Brad's case, he could have not exchanged numbers with the woman he had met. Perhaps meeting her frequently and having her help him during training was a bad decision; one that led to them falling in love.

The point is that we all face tempting situations. It's the ability to mitigate the events that follow that makes a difference. Think about the story I told you earlier about the guy climbing the tree to find his wife cheating on him. Love makes us do the craziest things. Love has the ability to overtake your reason and will blind you to the world in which you actually live. Brad is a perfect example; he was blind to the fact that he was married. That is why the relationship with his girlfriend began in the first place. When he first met her, the feeling of "new love" was overwhelming, and his marriage never even crossed his mind. His peers of course, not being blinded by these feelings, saw the situation clearly and reminded him daily of the realities of his life. If your friends or family are telling you something that might seem logical but that you really don't want to believe, then perhaps you need to take a second look to see if it's, in fact, ALL of them that have it wrong, or perhaps just you.

It's much easier to not put yourself in a bad situation than it is to get out of one. Brad and his wife had that initial flame at one point. Otherwise, they probably wouldn't have gotten married. Had Brad focused his attention on rekindling that flame, perhaps the outcome would have been much different. Even if that was not a possibility, at least he would end that marriage and have a clean slate to begin new with. Today's society now days makes it very easy, and almost encourages us to just give up and move on to the next best thing. You have to choose for yourself what you believe in; then fight for it. You also have to know when to move on and let things go, a very fine line to walk indeed. The nature of our careers makes it that much more difficult because you do find yourself away from home and away from those who hold you accountable for your actions. With that being said, you are who you are, regardless of what career you are in, so stay true to yourself. You may just find that you actually are or could be happy in your existing relationship.

CHAPTER 8
The Little Ones

"Children learn more from what you are than what you teach."

W.E.B Du Bois

Having children can be the most rewarding and joyful experience in your life. I often hear how hard it must be for me to be away from home with small children at home. Are you kidding me? Of course it is. It's hard enough as it is when you are gone from your spouse, now add your kids. The universe is funny how it plays out silly games on us. You can be home for 10 days and everything goes smoothly and without a hiccup. Then the day you walk out the door to leave on a trip, everything starts to fall apart. The dishwasher leaks, the air conditioner breaks, the car won't start... the list goes on, but regardless, they usually always happen while you are away. I cannot emphasize enough how important it is to have a solid and independent spouse at home.

Kids, on the other hand, are completely dependent on you, for everything. In this career, almost guaranteed, you will miss birthdays, holidays, special occasions, and sporting events. But instead of focusing on the negatives, let's look at the positives. How many parents are home for the entire day multiple days in in a row? In addition, when we leave work, we leave work there. All of our attention is at home and with our loved ones. Often, we have an entire week off at a time, perhaps can go on trips together and travel. If you had a stopwatch and timed the time you actually are at home, you will almost always have off more time than the guy next door working a regular 9-5 job. It's not the time spent away from your kids that matters; it's how you spend your time when you are with them. If you can remember just that, it will make a huge difference. Your kids need to have their parents around, but now days with modern technology, we are almost always reachable via voice or even camera. Some families place the camera right on his or her usual chair and eat dinner with the family. They can interact, talk, tell stories and laugh together with their families, no matter where they are physically located. You can call your kids and tell them bedtime stories, sing a nighttime lullaby, and then see them when they wake up. Of course this is not the same as seeing them in person, but it's a pretty good alternative if away from home.

POSTCARD JOURNAL

There are so many ways to show your children that you think about them while away. One guy I know sends a postcard to his kids from every city he visits, even if it's the same city multiple times. He dates the card and writes down what is going on in their lives at that time, kind of like a journal. At home, the kids place these cards in a special box and collect them. He figures that one day they will grow up and have a journal written on the back of postcards of their own life, something that not only tells them about their own life growing up, but that he always thought of them no matter where he was.

LITTLE KIDS DON'T KNOW ANY BETTER

Oftentimes, being gone from your kids is actually much harder for you than it is for them. They are busy in their daily lives, leaving little time to think about missing you. When the kids are very little, they are too busy exploring the world and learning how to walk and talk. The benefit of being that little is that they only know that kind of relationship with you. You being gone days at a time is normal to them. They cannot miss what they do not know. Of course when the kids are at that age, it's always more difficult for you and your spouse. You miss them and want to be home with them, while your spouse is left with all the work alone. When the kids get older, you still miss them, but at that point, they are busy in their own world and involved in being socially active. Again, focus on the time you have with them more than the time you don't have with them.

With that being said, it's obvious that the dynamic of your entire life changes when you introduce children into it. Assuming you were in this career prior to being married, you were gone from home for a period of time and then came home. Often, the time on the road was much more exciting than being home, so you would work more. Then you meet your spouse and suddenly you want to spend more time at home. You miss each other when you are away, but absence makes the heart grow fonder so you deal with the bad and look forward to the good. But then kids get involved, and everything changes. Before that point, your spouse was independent and dealt with things while you were away (so I hope at least). Kids are 100 percent reliant on you and your spouse. Think about infants; they would not survive if you didn't take care of them, period. Their survival depends on your ability to see to their needs and make sure they have what they need to live.

THE PARENT CONUNDRUM

This is where the conundrum begins for those of us who travel for a living. You naturally want to be home as much as possible to spend time with your kids. On one hand, you want to be physically present to raise the kids. On the other hand, you want to provide for them and your family. Unfortunately, the profession we have chosen does not allow both to occur at the same time.

When you are home with your kids, you are there to raise them, but at the same time, you are not providing for them. When you are providing for them, you are not physically there to raise them. To find balance between these two worlds is the key to happy parenting in this industry. Knowing that when you are away from home, you are actually providing for your kids makes you feel a little better, but of course, it doesn't mean you miss them any less. For the kids, what matters is that they know that you are there. By "there," I don't necessary mean physically, but rather emotionally. They need to know that you are part of their life, at home, or while away on a trip.

One of the pilots I interviewed sends his family a text from every hotel he visits with the local phone number and his room number. He also keeps his phone on while traveling overseas so that they can reach him if needed. His family also has the phone number to the company, and therefore, could technically reach him at any time, even if that means the company would notify the airplane enroute. Of course, they don't usually call him at these locations, but the fact that they know they could, if they wanted to, makes all the difference in the world. It bridges the gap of physical and emotional connection, something children cling to dearly.

Being Actually Present

When at home, make sure you are actually present, not just physically but also emotionally. Playing catch with your kid while you are talking or texting on your phone does not count for this. This is one of the great things about our jobs - we can leave work at work. Typically, when we come home from a trip, we have no work that we must do, and we can give our families our full attention. I have friends who work regular jobs, who come home from work, and then right after dinner, they hop on the computer to finish up last minute emails from the day and prepare for the events to come the next day. Not only are they gone all day, their work follows them home.

Recently, I was watching my 3-year-old at his gymnastics class. The gymnastics center is huge, and there are kids there from all ages, each at different stages in their training. Some of the talent there is incredible, seeing these young kids fly around the room flipping and twisting makes me dizzy just watching. My son was doing an exercise with his class across the gym from where I was, he couldn't have been any further away from where I was sitting. I watched him jump around like a monkey and then sit down next to his classmates waiting for his next turn. He looked right at me and gave me a quick thumbs up. That little connection we shared at that moment was an instant acknowledgment of my presence and him knowing that I was watching him. He just wanted to know that I was there and actually present, no matter where he was in the gym center. Giving your full, undivided attention goes a long way in his little world, which is a crucial element to your relationship with your children.

ATTENTION

Your kids will grow older and older, and will continue to seek attention and acknowledgment. The best place for this is with you and your spouse, but if you fail to do so, then they will begin to seek it in other places. Sometimes these other places are not so good, and that's when kids start to go down the wrong path, associating themselves with the wrong crowd. They do this simply because they are getting the attention they need from that group, bad or good. Kids will get your attention; if it's not through a good channel, then they will act badly if that means getting your full attention. For example, when children are extremely young they often times bite. They do this because they don't know how else to communicate with you; they do this to express frustration. Bottom line, kids figure out a way to get their point across, and sometimes it's not an ideal or painless method. You can make it an easier process by adapting to their level of communication and need.

ISLAND LIFE

One of the most positive and uplifting stories I remember was one of a Captain who lived in Tampa, Florida. Shelton grew up on the U.S. Virgin Island of St. Thomas. He met his wife Mia back when they were growing up on the island. Their families were close friends, and they belonged to the same church. Shelton started his aviation career loading fruits and vegetables on and off a DC-3 that was flying between the Islands and San Juan, Puerto Rico. The owners of the company recognized his hard work ethic, and he soon was allowed to jumpseat on some of the out and back flights. He loved being in the cockpit and quickly fell in love with flying.

He started taking flying lessons, but it took him a long time to earn his pilots licenses since it was extremely expensive. Shelton continued to work hard and used all of his hard earned money to pay for more flying lessons, finally earning all of his ratings. He eventually got a job flying in the right seat of a small charter outfit that primarily shuttled cruise ship passengers and tourists between San Juan to the various Caribbean Islands. The weather was usually nice and they would fly from sunrise to sunset. He built his flight hours very quickly and was soon hired to fly for a large mainland regional airline based in San Juan. During this time, Mia was working for her family's local produce business. Typically, she would see Shelton Friday and Saturday nights. Their courtship was a lovely time, and they would enjoy nice walks and picnics on the beach watching the sunset.

Life was good for the two, and Shelton had been secretly saved for an engagement ring ever since he got his first job loading and unloading the cargo planes. One day while Mia was at work, Shelton visited her parents and asked for their blessing to ask for Mia's hand in marriage. They had known him since he was a little boy, so they were filled with joy that he would marry their daughter. Shelton and Mia had a lovely beach wedding, and then moved to San Juan to start their life together. They were pretty tight on money and could only afford rent for a small apartment. Since they were used to living on a small island, however, the apartment was plenty big for the two of them.

A year later, Shelton began to apply for jobs flying for some bigger airlines and received a job offer from a large airline based in the United States. The money was very good, and although he would miss the island flying, he was excited to start a new job flying bigger airplanes. Mia had an uncle who lived in Tampa, Florida and having never lived so far from home, they figured they could live there while Shelton commuted to work. They bought a small home and quickly met a lot of great people who became great friends.

FROM POVERTY TO LUXURY

It wasn't too long after the move that Mia was pregnant with their first child. The next thing they knew, they had a nice little family living in a lovely home, and their second quickly joined their first son. They visited their families at least once a year, and when the kids got a little older, they traveled on at least three annual vacations. They lived very frugally, and since they never had much growing up, they never missed anything.

Shelton figured saving money on material things and spending it on vacationing was much more valuable in life, not just to him and Mia but also more importantly, to his two sons. They would grow up seeing the world, both nice places and also very poor parts of the world. They would go on at least one luxurious trip a year, and then took one trip to volunteer at a very poor country or island. They saw how good things are in some parts of the world, and then saw how poor others were. His sons were not only able to see the world but also build an appreciation for the nice places by having seen the poor places. This, Shelton figured, was one of the greatest values a person today could have. Too many kids now grow up spoiled and blind to the realities of the world. Things are taken for granted and expected, rather than earned. His relationship with Mia was better than ever and they enjoyed raising their two boys.

Twenty years later, they were still living in the same home, both boys had full scholarships to good universities, and the relationship they had with their sons was amazing. Shelton considered himself the luckiest husband to have married such an amazing woman, and the luckiest dad to be blessed by his two sons. He never got caught up in the rat race of buying newer and bigger things, teaching his sons early to earn the things they enjoyed. When I asked him what the challenges were raising his kids in this society, he said the fact that Mia and he were raised by a humble hard working family on a relatively poor island, made it difficult to show his sons how that life was compared to their own.

His sons would watch television and see how society was living and then would go to school and see other kids with their newest gadgets and toys. He said the most valuable and rewarding thing he did raising his kids was to spend so much time traveling. He said that no matter what you tell your kids or what they watch on TV, having them actually experience another culture in person taught them so many life lessons that shaped them to be such great kids. When you see things for yourself like poverty and hunger, then you start not to take things for granted in life. You realize the value of the dollar and that earning things in life is much more rewarding than just receiving them. This is a lesson that more kids should learn in today's world.

GREATEST REGRET

Not to get off topic too much, but here is something to consider in your personal life in regards to your faithfulness to your spouse and having children. If you are unfaithful and cheat on your spouse, you will not only hurt them, but also lose all respect from them. If you do this and also have children, you also lose the respect from your own children. One Captain I spoke with said that his biggest regret in life was having an affair while married to his wife, which eventually led to a divorce. It wasn't the hurt he caused his wife, although he did feel terrible about that, it was how it hurt his kids that bothered him the most.

His kids were younger when the affair took place. They couldn't really understand why mommy and daddy were separating. But then, when the kids got older, he eventually had to tell them that the reason they split up was because daddy couldn't keep his pants on while away on the road. Not only did he feel so ashamed to tell them that, but he also lost the respect from his own children. Why would they ever come to him for relationship advice in the future? What did they think of his moral character after learning this? What if they turned out like him and did the same in their own life? He regretted this more than anything in his life and said that if he could offer any advice to anyone reading this book, it was to think of his story.

Think of your kids and how you will one day have to explain to them why you did what you did and why you didn't try harder to keep the marriage intact by staying faithful. The Captain said the fact that you are married should keep you from having an affair in the first place, but if not for that alone, then your kids should certainly be reason enough. Something to think about the next time you face with temptation or find yourself in a similar situation. Thinking of the end often times changes the beginning.

CHAPTER 9
Reality Check

"Reality is merely an illusion, albeit a very persistent one."
Albert Einstein

One of the most dangerous attributes of our type of personality is how we view reality. There is the reality that is actually real, and then there is the reality that is what we would like it to be. Unfortunately, the two are not always the same, at least not in our perception. When we go through pilot training, we learn to deal with reality and the perception of reality. Seeing things the way they really are versus the way you would like to see them. This is critical in analyzing situations, especially in emergencies. If you are flying along and your engine catches on fire, then the reality is that the engine is on fire. You cannot think to yourself how inconvenient that is, or perhaps it's a false indication, maybe it's not really that bad... this is often a big player in bad weather flying. You are on the last day of your trip, last flight home and have a big wedding to go to when you get there. The weather report shows a line of thunderstorms between you and your final destination, what a mess. You really want, and need to get back home. So you start looking at the radar more, trying to see if there are any holes you might be able to squeeze through. Is the weather really that bad or is it just heavy rain. Perhaps it will die down by the time you get to it and then you will still have a chance to make it home in time. Maybe you can fly over the storms and visually pick your way through the tops of the clouds. What about a mechanical issue? How many times have you had a mechanical problem on the final flight home of a long exhausting trip that has gone flawless up to this point? You cannot believe it's happening and start to think about how bad it could really be. Can't we just fix it later? Can't we just say it broke during the flight home and they can deal with it after we land? All those factors have and will happen to all of us, it is up to us to differentiate between the actual reality and the reality we want to believe.

HOW BAD CAN IT REALLY BE?

This same concept applies to our daily lives. We are constantly battling actual reality and perceived reality. Think at the last time you were at the doctor's office. You sit there eagerly waiting for the doctor; you nervously think of every possible scenario and actually begin to stress about them. What if I have cancer, a rare disease, or something that's contagious... but in reality it could be something entirely different. With that being said, what if you go for a routine checkup and discover that you have a serious illness, will you deny the severity at first refusing to accept the reality of the situation? The first step in dealing with bad news or a loss is denial. This is a significant factor in our line of work; as we cannot let that natural tendency, to deny a reality, influence our actions in response.

Why is this a big deal for us? Your relationship is what you make of it, but you must see it for what it is and not for what you wish it to be. For example, what if you are dating someone who has serious trust issues? The reality is that in this job you solely rely on faithfulness and trust, otherwise you will drive yourself and your partner crazy. You wish the reality were different because that way you can justify the relationship. Accepting reality in this instance might mean that you are not well suited for one another. They might think you are being unfaithful or deceitful, but in reality you could be very honest and trustworthy. The perceived realities can overcome the actual realities and change your perception of the situation to match that of what you think it is. If you think about something long and hard enough, you might actually believe that it is true. Mark Twain said, "Reality can be beaten with enough imagination." This can have devastating consequences in a relationship and therefore you need to be aware of this reality check. See the reality for what it really is and not for what you would like it to be.

I recently interviewed a pilot who wanted to fly internationally and travel the world. He married a homebody girl who loved to be close to home. The actual reality was that their goals in life were different and not at all compatible, but the desired reality blinded them to overlook that. The same goes for couples that meet and fall madly in love. Perhaps one of them wants to have lots of children but the other does not.

They both figure that once married they will figure things out, just to find out later that their common goals are not compatible. The reality was always right in front of them, they just failed to accept it and clung on to a perceived reality that allowed them to continue the relationship. Sometimes accepting the reality of things does not produce the desired outcome in the short term, but in the long run it is also the inevitable outcome.

"HONEY, HOW CAN I HELP?"

Cultural differences are also a big part of our perceived realities. To give you an example, I knew a guy once who was dating a girl in Thailand. He had been living there for a few years and fell in love with the pristine beaches and wonderful people. One day, she made him a nice lunch and afterward he picked up his plate and brought it to the kitchen. When he came back to the table he noticed his girlfriend was in tears. He had no idea why, and after a few minutes she went on to explain to him what he had done. He put his own plate in the kitchen, something that her culture believes she should do herself. She felt inadequate and felt so bad about him doing that. He had absolutely no intention of upsetting her and would have never thought that this type of behavior even existed. Having lived in the States for most of his life he never lived in a culture like the one she came from. She felt inadequate where in reality he was just trying to help out. Unnecessary tears were shed where they didn't have to be, but that's where communication comes in, and once understood, can be mitigated in the future.

The Time Zone Effect

The reason I tell the story about this guy in Thailand, is because I want to tell you about the "time zone effect." I'm not even sure what to call this but some people seem to think that once they are a certain number of time zones away from home, they are free to do whatever they want. Marital vows, commitments, responsibilities, all get thrown out the window and they become like kids in a candy store. This happens all over the world but even more noticeably in poorer countries. Let's examine why that is for a minute.

I have personally flown with guys who spend hours on end complaining about their spouses at home. A friend of mine once explained to me that some cultures, especially the Asian ones, are much more service oriented than ours. I can't speak from personal experience with regard to relationships, but in the airline customer service, that fact is clearly obvious. So when these guys I am talking about fly overseas to Asia for example, mingle with the local crowd, they suddenly feel like those people all have the qualities that their spouses lack. They think to themselves that this is so much better than dealing with things back at home, why not just divorce their spouse and marry a local woman from over here? Many of them throw away years and years of marriage, just to get remarried and start a new life with the person that they feel meets all of their needs. Then they bring them back home and are surprised when they are divorced a few years later. To make things even worse, on average the age difference between the guy and the local girl is often 20-30 years, I have even seen 40+ years. Please don't take this the wrong way, and I know there is always an exception, but what are the odds that a 20-year-old girl from a small village in Thailand wants to marry a 63-year-old pilot from the States for true love? Again, I am not judging, but this to me seems like there are other motives at play here. Especially considering that once the minimum time is met for a foreigner to live in the States without being married anymore, a divorce is often imminent. Doesn't that seem a little too convenient to be just bad luck for these couples?

The perceived reality here is that the man thinks that she is attracted to him for who he is and will love him through thick and thin. He doesn't think there is anything wrong with this picture and his friends that have gone through the same situation, but got divorced, just made mistakes that he won't make. The reality is that she, most likely at least, is looking for a better life than what she had at home and this guy is her way out. She doesn't really love this man in the same sense, and so once she can safely stay in the States without him, can divorce the guy and start her new life from scratch. After all, she perhaps would like to have children of her own.

I once worked with a guy who was getting married to a South American woman, very attractive and just turned 20. He was 60 and his two daughters were in their late 20s. I was with them when he introduced his daughters to their new stepmom, you can imagine how awkward that was for everyone (interestingly enough it didn't seem to bother the guy much at all). They got married, moved to Atlanta, and after exactly three years, divorced. Think about the reality of the situation. She would be 45, ready to travel the world and enjoy life, while he would be luckily to even be alive at age 85. Perhaps in 10 years she would like to have kids. So she would be 30, a good age to have kids after all, and he would now have a newborn and be 70 years old himself.

However, I have also flown with a guy who is married to a woman 40 years younger than him, and they appear truly happy together, recently welcoming their first child to their family. For some it works out, but many simply refuse to accept the reality of the fact that this setup is doomed to fail from the beginning. Reality is what it is, it's much easier to accept it than to try to force things to be that simply cannot be.

Again, I am not saying that all of these relationships are for the wrong reasons, but many of them appear to be. The reason I am telling you this is because I think it is important to keep focus on the reality of the situation you are in. If you are having a hard time at home and are away, perhaps even in tempting situations, keep in mind that the reality, which you perceive, may be skewed by your emotions caused by your issues at home. Before acting on those, step back and think about what is really going on and perhaps you will act differently when you can see the reality for what it truly is.

"You can avoid reality, but you cannot avoid the consequences of avoiding reality."

Ayn Rand

CHAPTER 10
Who's In Charge?

"He that can have patience can have what he will."
Benjamin Franklin

The aviation industry is very much like Disney World. It's unique and special, lots of people want to go there and it costs an arm and a leg to get in. Once inside, there are lots of fun rides and roller coasters. Space Mountain, where you sit in a cart and go through ups and downs, blinded by darkness, never knowing what will happen next, best resembles an aviation career. You never know what to expect, those that don't know, do all the talking; those that do know, don't. The kids love the food at Disney because it's exciting to eat there, but us adults would rather eat nothing and save $19 you'll pay for a pizza shaped like a Mickey Mouse. Take a family of five from Europe who wants to visit Disney. They have to buy five international airline tickets, pay for nights in the hotel, and then top that off with Disney passes that aren't cheap. Not to mention food and time off work, this trip is expensive. With that being said, it takes a certain type of individual to plan for this trip. Work hard, save money, plan the trip, get time off, make all the bookings, the list goes on.

Aviation is very similar, not everyone can do it. It doesn't matter if you are working in the aviation industry or travel for work, you are away from home and often times stay away for weeks at a time. You deal with jet leg, weather, delays, industry cuts, layoffs, long periods of training, relocation, commuting... it takes a certain type of individual to stick with it and stay in the industry. With that being said, our job requires us to exhibit certain personalities and characteristics that allow us to perform our duties efficiently.

Lights, Camera, Action

Let's take a look at Mike and Jim from the previous chapters, both successful Captains at big airlines. Both were willing to give up their lives for a country they believed in, both went through months of testing and training. When they were given a jet that could fly at over the speed of sound, loaded with weapons that could take out an entire city, they were put in charge. When we fly airplanes, or are part of a crew, we are basically actors in a play. We have a script, we learn and memorize it, and then we go perform. Rarely do circumstances call for us to totally venture off the script. The nice thing with that is that we know what to expect from others, and they of us. When you are the Captain or the lead Purser of a flight, you set the tone and are in charge, people look up to you for guidance, and not much goes on without you being informed of it. We also operate on a tight schedule, often minutes make the difference for hundreds of passengers making or missing a connecting flight. We don't show up to the airport, pick a random plane, hop on, and after take off figure out where we are headed. Precise planning goes into our daily lives from fuel calculations, weather reports and wind charts, to crew duty times. We know what we are scheduled to do for the entire trip, down to the minute.

OFF THE CLOCK

Let's consider a typical trip, say 10 days around the world. Every leg is carefully planned out for you; you know when you are leaving and when you are arriving. At the end of your trip you fly back home and get in your car to drive home. You feel tired, your clothes are worn and dirty, you desperately need a shower and then you finally arrive at your home. You walk in the door, there are the kids excited to see you and your wife happy as well because now she finally gets a well-deserved break (plus she is excited to see you too, you hope). You get caught up with the mail, play with the kids, clean up, and go to bed. You wake up the next morning and now what? You have had everything planned out for the past 10 days, knew what time you would leave and arrive, and now you are home and free to do whatever you want. Sure you have your schedules and routines, but does it matter if you leave the driveway at 8 or at 8:10. Will that require you to fill out a report explaining the 10-minute delay?

You see the laundry in the dirty clothes hamper, and immediately put the clothes in the wash. You feel good about it because you like getting things done that need to be done, but deep down you wonder why it wasn't done already. You then unload the dishwasher, again happy that it's empty now and there is room for the dirty dishes, but once again deep down you wonder why you are having to do this.

Here is where one of the greatest challenges stems from in our lives. Our personality is driven on planning, seeing things that need to be done and doing them. Why wait to do something, like throw the dirty clothes in the wash, if you can just do it now. For most of us it is difficult to walk by something that you know needs to be done, but that's just our personality. You have been gone for 10 days and everything is fine, the kids are fed, the house hasn't fallen apart, and the kids are wearing clean clothes. So obviously things get done just fine, just not necessarily on your schedule. Your spouse has been in charge while you were away the entire time, setting the tone, doing the disciplining, making sure everything gets done. We often times come home, and since we have been in charge for the past 10 days, feel like that can continue at home. But I've got news for you, that just simply doesn't work. It's not fair to your spouse, not fair to the kids, and not fair to you.

WHO IS RUNNING THE SHOW HERE?

During my interview with Jim and Mike, I found this trait to be present in both relationships. Both said that when they came home they would take charge and try to run the show. Their kids knew that now daddy was home and now his rules applied. They also knew that when daddy goes to work, mommy's rules were back in play, and they would adjust to them once he left. Both Mike and Jim's wives said that it was so frustrating to have their husbands come home because they would have their own schedule to get things done, and the minute they walked in the door they would take over. Then to top things off, they could sense the disappointment in their husbands and that would make them frustrated. Instead of the husband focusing on what a great job they did the entire time they were gone, they would focus on the things that weren't done when they expected them to be done. The women both said that they would run things just fine when their husbands were gone away on trips. Sure the laundry would pile up on certain days, or the dishwasher wouldn't run every day, but things got done and after all, taking care of kids and a household is the hardest job anyone could have. The husbands both said that they felt like they would have to work while away, and then also have to work while at home. In Jim's case, his wife felt so bad about him not showing her his appreciation that she ended up finding it with someone else. Of course that's not an excuse for cheating on your partner, but it's what happened.

"LOOK AT ME DAD"

It's similar with families that have multiple kids. Let's say the older of two is doing great in school and is a super star on his high school football team. At home he is constantly praised and acknowledged for his hard work and success. The younger kid is always around when his older brother gets praised, but he himself is not so good at sports. He is however, the nicest kid in the class and is the next chess champion of the world. If the dad is a huge sports jock, then he will likely pay more attention to the older kid because they have more in common. The younger kid might feel left out and will start looking to get attention in other ways. Positive or negative, rest assured that they will get attention. Often times the child who gets less attention becomes the trouble kid who gets himself involved in the wrong crowd and breaks the rules more. This is because it's an easy path to attention; anyone can be a loser if you just quit trying. Just take a look in the news now a days, horrific shootings in schools all around the country. Most of these kids involved in masterminding these terrible acts were not on the football team all-star list. Some have even written in letters that this would finally get them noticed, or that nobody would know they were gone. Obviously we are discussing something on an entirely different magnitude here, but what I am saying is that humans seek attention, and they will get it either through good or bad actions.

"HONEY, YOU LOOK BEAUTIFUL TONIGHT"

If a woman needs to hear that she looks pretty and that makes her feel good, then she will hear it. The question is, if it's the husband telling her what she needs to hear or whether it's someone outside of his or her marriage. There is a great book written by Gary Chapman called *Love Languages*, I highly recommend this book to anyone. It's not only great for romantic relationships, but also great for relationships with your kids.

In our earlier story, Jim's wife was relocated to a new state, had no friends, didn't know her way around, and was left by herself with the kids for long periods of time. When Jim came home, he would be busy fishing and enjoying the fruits that Alaska had to offer, but he failed to be there for his wife. When he was out on the road he was absent, then when he was home he would remain absent, never truly being present. She eventually found someone to be there for her, but unfortunately it wasn't Jim.

HANDLING THE PRESSURE

We have had to adapt to these qualities in our lives in order to survive in this industry. For pilots, we have had to spend thousands and thousands of dollars to go to flight school, take countless tests and memorize more numbers than we thought possible. We have to become actors in which the script is an operations manual, and we have a part in this giant production. The only difference is that if we forget a line at the wrong time, we either fail a check ride and will have to suffer from that the rest of our careers, or we damage an airplane or worse.

At my previous flying job the pressure was so high that they actually had a bar near the training center that was nicknamed "the slasher bar." This was because after failing a check ride, an individual was so upset, that he tried to slash his wrists in the restroom. It's been years since I have worked at that company but I can still remember the callouts and procedures like it was yesterday, that's how much I studied. Every check ride was a career ride and your one single performance would determine your entire lifetime career there.

Talking about pressure, holy cow. So with that being said, we studied like crazy and all helped each other out since we were in the same boat. To make matters worse, we were away from home for six months straight during training so again juggling home life with our professional life. You couldn't call home and complain to your wife that you had to sit in the coffee shop for eight hours today with earplugs in, reading manuals, while your wife was at home dealing with a newborn, a 3-year-old, and the house. It took motivation, determination, and lots of studying to pass all of these hurdles. We all have to go through this, perhaps not all to that level of extreme, but nonetheless difficult stages in the career path. The qualities that this takes are great for the job we do, but absolutely not conducive to a healthy relationship at home.

JUST GO ALONG WITH IT

If you go to work, no matter who you are paired to fly with, the cockpit procedures are pretty much the same every time. If you spend four days on a trip, each day will run pretty much the same in the cockpit as far as procedures go. However, spend four days at home and you don't know if you will sleep two hours straight, if the 4-year-old decides to water everything in the bathroom minus the toilet in the middle of the night, or the teenage daughter comes home two hours past her curfew. Your entire life is changed; you go from being part of a well thought out play, to complete chaos. You might think you have it all in control, and that's about the time life throws you a curve ball.

What if Jim and Mike came home from their trips and just simply went along with things? Instead of coming home and running the show like they may at work, they simply went along with the way things have been running smoothly for the past few days. What if they came home, asked their wives what they could help with, and then made dinner for everyone? "Honey, you have done an amazing job while I have been gone and I can only imagine how exhausted you must be. You look beautiful and I love you so much, you are an amazing woman and I am so thankful to have married such an incredible woman." Now you might read this and think I am an idiot, but what if they had said that once in a while, instead of coming home and being upset that the dishes were dirty and laundry wasn't done? This may not sound like a big deal once or twice, but it all adds up, and over time can cause irreversible damage in a relationship. Jim's wife said that if she had felt more appreciated, even just once in a while, things would have been much different. Feeling like a disappointment in your own house, by the one person who is supposed to love you more than anyone, is so hurtful.

EXPONENTIAL GROWTH

We are so focused on compounding interest in our retirement account, why would this be any different. You plant a little thought and appreciation in your marriage, and it will grow exponentially over time. The same is true for the opposite; as you plant a seed of doubt or disappointment, it will grow over time as well and the result is that you will become another statistic for failed marriages. Jim and Mike both said that looking back at their marriages, had they shown a little more appreciation towards their wives, things would have been much different. The wives said the same thing. So there you have it, take it for what it's worth but a little bit here and there goes a long way.

> *"What is emotional intimacy? It is that deep sense of being connected to one another. It is feeling loved, respected and appreciated, while at the same time seeking to reciprocate. To feel loved is to have the sense that the other person genuinely cares about your well-being. Respect has to do with feeling that your potential spouse has positive regard for your personhood, intellect, abilities and personality. Appreciation is that inner sense that your partner values your contribution to the relationship."*

> *Gary Chapman, Love Languages*

CHAPTER 11
Foreign Lands

"Obstacles are those frightful things you see when you take your eyes off your goals."

Henry Ford

Tim was one of the youngest pilots at one of the major regionals. He was eager to be there and loved flying. This whole airline thing was new to him and he was just excited to finally be paid to fly for a change instead of paying to fly. He lived in Cleveland where he was based and had a small house there near the airport. If you walked into his house you would find models of airplanes painted in all different colors, but the one common theme was that they were all big planes from international airlines that often hired Americans. He knew that one day he wanted to join one of these global airlines and fly big planes all around the world.

One day, he met up with some friends at a local bowling alley. There they ran into another group of mutual friends, one of them being a young woman he had gone to high school with. Her name was Gina and he remembered her well as they had a few classes together. She was a teacher at a small school in town, loved her job, and dreamed of living close to home raising a nice family. Tim and Gina fell madly in love, within a few months they were engaged and planning a big wedding for the following spring. They were so excited to spend the rest of their lives together. Gina was also very close to her family and they would spend numerous nights a week eating dinner together. Tim got along great with her parents and felt like family right from the beginning. A nice wedding followed and they began their journey through life together.

DREAMS DO COME TRUE

Tim had always sent applications to all the airlines to show interest and it became a hobby to update them every few months. Gina never thought much of this, as she found it highly unrealistic for him to get hired to fly such a big jet. After all, he was currently flying a small regional jet. Well one day he received a phone call from one of the fastest growing airlines in the world based in Dubai. Their smallest plane was bigger than most domestic airlines' planes and the thought of him finally landing his dream job was overwhelming. He prepared diligently for the interview and did whatever he could to study. Gina was very supportive and helped him prepare by quizzing him and picking out the perfect interview suit, but still was not too worried about actually having to move anywhere. He arrived at the interview and joined the other candidates in the waiting room. All were dressed in suits, carried shiny briefcases, all set to impress. While they were waiting they started talking about where they were from and what airlines they were currently working for. Most of them were much more qualified than he was, so he felt a little intimidated by the competition interviewing that day. He completed the interview process and headed home to his wife. He had no idea what to expect next, but knew that if he passed the first interview, they would fly him and his spouse out to Dubai for the second interview. A few days passed and finally he received a phone call from human resources, inviting him to the second interview.

Amazing, could this really be happening. Gina saw how excited her husband was, and knowing that this was his dream, she agreed to fly with him to Dubai for his second interview. She had reservations right from the beginning because she really didn't think much of living in the Middle East. Hollywood and the news have skewed the perception of that region, but she also knew that you really have to go for yourself to see what it is really like. I can't speak much about most of the Middle East, but Dubai is an incredible city where if it weren't so hot in the summer you would never know you were in the middle of the desert. Deep down, Gina felt that he wouldn't actually get the job. So she went through the motions and figured, if nothing else, they would get a free trip to Dubai. The interview went much better than Tim expected and Gina seemed to enjoy visiting Dubai more than she thought she would.

They arrived back home and went back to their normal lives for the time being. Tim was eager to hear about the results of his final interview. Meanwhile she was just happy to be back from their little vacation. A few weeks later the big news came, he was hired. Finally his dreams became a reality and he would be flying a big wide body jet all around the world. Upon hearing the news, Gina immediately began to cry. Fear and doubt flooded her emotions and the reality set in that their lives, as they knew it, were about to change. Gina was a homebody. She loved being close to home and her family, and the thought of leaving all of this was terrifying to her. During their visit to Dubai they were told that most schools for the expatriate families hired English-speaking teachers, so she would have no problem finding a job to keep busy. She figured it might actually be good for her resume to have some international teaching experience; surely they wouldn't live there too long anyway. Reluctant at first, Gina finally agreed to give it a try.

FROM HAMBURGERS TO HUMMUS AND TABBOULEH

Tim's initial training would start in a few months, which gave them just enough time to sell their house and belongings, spend a few more weeks at home with family, and then it was off to Dubai. They had a choice, to either live in a company provided apartment, or receive a housing allowance and pick out their own residence. They chose the latter and found a nice little apartment near the water. The airline hired mostly expats from all around the world, so there were lots of families in similar situations as Tim and his wife; strangers living in a strange new city. Customs in the Middle East are much different than back in the States and this took a little getting used to for Gina. Training went quick and the two were able to spend lots of time together since he was home every night. She stayed busy furnishing the apartment and making it a cozy place to come home to. Tim bought a nice used car, a

Mercedes. They noticed that the front window had a big tinted area on the top half of the windshield. Then on the side of the window there was a rolled up shade that you could span across the bottom half of the windshield. Confused, Tim and Gina asked the car sales associate why this was installed, not sure why you would want the entire front windshield tinted really dark. That's when it was explained to them that the previous owner didn't want people to see his wife when she was driving. Gina had never heard of such a thing, it was her first experience with a new culture with customs she had only read about in books.

Tim finished his check ride and now the fun part started. He would finally be flying all over the world. Gina quickly found herself in the new apartment alone while Tim was out flying to new exotic destinations. They had been together during training and since they chose to find their own place to live in, there weren't as many expats to mingle with as they mainly chose the company provided housing. Even short three-day trips seemed to last forever for her, the time alone began to eat at her. She was homesick, missed her family, her home, her life the way it was before. To make matters even worse, Tim would occasionally get trips back to the States and would visit friends they had together, but again she was stuck back in Dubai all alone. The airline Tim was working for took great pride in customer service and it recruited lots of cabin crew from all around the world. So not only was Tim now flying to exotic places all around the globe, he was also doing that with 20 lively cabin crew from all parts of the world.

Loneliness and jealousy began to eat at Gina more and more; eventually she couldn't take it anymore. She bought a ticket and flew home. Not really having a set plan, she figured she would go back and after a few weeks would return to Dubai to get the homesick part out of her system.

LET ME GO

A few weeks turned into a few months, and finally Gina flew back to Dubai to discuss their future together. In the meantime, Tim was happier than ever working at his dream job, so quitting and moving back to the States was not an option for him. Gina on the other hand was not willing to stay in Dubai and be miserable any longer. They loved each other very much, and to their credit, handled this part very responsibly. They loved each other enough to let go of the relationship, knowing that they would be much happier apart. They drew up a fair and mutually agreeable divorce plan. Few assets were left to deal with since they sold most of it before moving to Dubai. After a quick trip to the US embassy, who would notarize the paper, their young marriage ended. Gina moved back home and lived with her parents initially, happy to be back home again. At first Tim and Gina would talk frequently, but over time the conversations became shorter and shorter with more time in between calls, eventually coming to an end all together (there is a sour twist to this story, but we will get to that later in the book).

The moral of the story is that this job is not suitable for anyone or any relationship. For Tim and Gina, the relationship truly was doomed from the beginning. Ultimately, one of them would have been unhappy since their individual goals and expectations were not that of the others. One wanted to stay close to home, the other wanted to go out and explore the world, pretty much completely opposite from each other. Had Tim not taken the job, he would have held their marriage responsible for him not pursuing his dreams, which would have eaten at their relationship and caused unrepairable damages. If Gina would have stayed in Dubai, she would have sacrificed her own happiness to allow Tim to pursue his dreams. Again their marriage would have been held accountable for unhappiness and this would have eaten away at their relationship. To have common goals is key in any marriage, but especially in our career field since the change can be so drastic. Aviation is a global industry and so your next job could potentially take you anywhere on the planet. Some are happy to fly domestically all their lives; others only want to fly internationally. Many airlines offer both kinds of flying which is even better, but not everyone has the opportunity to land such a job. You have to find what works for you and your spouse, but be honest with each other and know what you are getting into before you actually sign up for it.

Having asked both Tim and Gina about their failed marriage, both said that they would not have gotten married in the first place if given the opportunity to do it over again. Blinded by new love, they disregarded their differences and future expectations out of life. They were sad that they lost their marriage, but more sad to have lost their friendship. Both were glad that they didn't have kids yet which made the separation easier. Gina confessed to silently hoping that that airline would not have hired Tim, but she felt guilty for feeling this way. How do you think they handled their situation? Should they not have gotten married knowing their differences in desires? What if he never got the interview in the first place, would that have changed things for them? Imagine had they tried to stick it out and continued to stay married, only to realize years later that it wasn't going to work out. Nothing comes for free and sometimes the price to pay for something is simply too high. Place a value on your own happiness and never short yourself of the opportunity to reach your goals, weather that's in your professional or personal life. Sacrifices will have to be made and only you can decide which are worth making.

"Dreams do come true, if only we wish hard enough. You can have anything in life if you will sacrifice everything else for it."

J.M Barrie

CHAPTER 12
Adapting To Change

"Best laid plans of mice and men often go astray."
Robert Burns

Part of earning your Pilot's license was to complete a long cross-country trip. The task had a list of requirements, which that flight had to meet, ranging from distance to how many landings your flight had to have. I had around 40 flight hours when I did my first long cross-country flight; I remember it like it was yesterday. I was living in central Florida and my flight would take me down to the Miami area, across the state to Ft. Myers, and then back to Orlando. This was a serious journey for me at that stage of my flight training, I felt like I was Columbus setting out to explore the world. I planned vigorously and had every single detail figured out. I was nervous that morning but felt comfortable with my planning and set out on the first leg. The flight went as planned, and upon landing in Miami, I checked the weather across the state, filled up the tanks, and off I went.

Leg two also went as planned, I started to feel much more comfortable and felt good about having spent so much time planning this trip. I landed uneventfully in Ft. Myers and once again checked the weather prior to my final leg home. There were a few rain showers north of Orlando but the storms usually didn't roll in until the late afternoon, well after I would land in Orlando. I filled the gas tanks again and set off for home, after all, my planning was spot on so far so what could go wrong.

POPCORN CLOUDS

I was just passing the half way mark when I noticed the dark clouds ahead. They surely didn't seem north of Orlando, and since I was headed north, I began to think that there might a problem. I called flight service and they advised me that the storm had really grown and was located between my position and Orlando, suggesting I would quickly turn around. Turn around? That was not in my planning. I planned every single bridge I would fly over, every lake I would use as references, but to fly somewhere where I hadn't been? Right then, rain that appeared out of nowhere, covered my windshield and I could barely see anything out the front window. I had never flown in rain so now panic set in. Could this really be happening, is this a dream or am I really in this situation? Needless to say my decision to turn around was made simple and the next thing I knew I was headed back south racing a storm that I had not planned for. The voice on the radio advised me to head toward a small little airport that was a few miles from where I was. He then gave me a phone number to call, which really made me even more nervous as I always thought if you really get in trouble, you get a phone number to call. I landed at the small airport, never having even heard of it, and then taxied to a small building that looked pretty deserted. I shut the engine down and just made it to the building before the sky opened up and buckets of water fell out.

As I walked inside I found a few vending machines, an office counter that looked like it hasn't been used in years, and a pay phone. I quickly and nervously called the number that the controller gave me and was very relieved to hear that he just wanted to make sure I made it on the ground safely. By now the rain had gotten so hard that I could almost not even see the plane on the ramp. A few hours went by and I was starting to get worried about what if the weather didn't improve before nightfall. After a few more hours of watching the sky dump lakes of water on my little Cessna, the rain subsided and it was time to head home. The flight back to Orlando went pretty uneventful, and even though I was back a few hours later than expected, I completed my long cross-country, which for me was a huge hurdle in earning my pilot's license.

Don't Be Afraid to Turn Around

The reason I tell this story is because even though you might plan out your entire future, things rarely go according to plan in life. Our job requires us to plan ahead, prepare for the worst, and hope for the best. We spend our entire career practicing things in the simulator that hopefully will never actually happen, and only a small percentage of us actually experience them in real life. We think of all the things that could go wrong in a flight, and then practice them over and over to the point where we can react to them naturally. It takes that type of personality to do this type of work and not everyone is cut out to be that way.

We are constantly aware of things like the time, or our position relative to where we need to be. It could be at the airport, in the air, or at the mall. Individuals with our personalities are usually always on-time if not a few minutes early. We tend to have at least one backup plan available at all times, and rarely find ourselves in positions where we have no clue what to do. We have show times, release times, departure times, enroute times, Bingo Fuel times, the list goes on. When you spend a few days in a row where usually everything is on some type of time control, then suddenly find yourself at home on the family time, things get interesting. Every family is different, but I know if my youngest is supposed to go to bed at 19:00, I don't like it if it's 19:30 and he is still monkeying around. I know that it won't hurt him, but it's the fact that I had planned on him in bed by 19:00 and it's not happening that makes me anxious. Life will never go exactly as planned, as no matter how well you plan things ahead, you will always encounter situations that require change. Of all the things I thought of and planned for on my long cross-country flight, I never thought of having to turn around and land where I did. What would have happened if I simply stayed hard-headed and pressed on. I didn't plan for it, so I am not going to give in. How do you think my little Cessna would have held up in a massive summer time Florida thunderstorm?

Depending on whom you talk to, some people might consider their relationship one of these storms, so why would you fly right into it. Adapt, think outside the box, and take the plan that will ensure your safety. If a situation is taking you right into a storm, why not deviate from what you originally planned and change the course. As easy as this sounds, our personalities do not make this decision easy. We fight battles at home that are certain to not end well, just to make a point or stay the course. You have to realize your limitations and act upon them. Know that it may not feel natural to deviate from the plan but sometimes situations call for that change. If I ask your spouse if you are stubborn, hard headed, or strong minded, what do you think he or she would say? If you just took life as it came and never made or stuck to plans, do you think you would have made it this far in your career? Who would you want to pilot your airplane your family was on, one that was able to adapt to change and recognize when change is required, or one that sticks to the plan no matter what? With that being said, you also don't want the pilot to be day dreaming in cartoons and spending most of their time in Lala Land, never looking more than one step ahead in life. But then again, that kind of person would not likely be up front in the first place.

So as you can see, there is a fine line between being motivated, determined, having the ability to plan ahead, and knowing when change or an alteration to the plan is required. When things don't go according to plan at home, and I promise they won't, take a step back and think about what the best solution is to deal with that situation. Sometimes doing a U-turn from the plan could be the best solution, I know it was for me that day on my flight.

Keep in mind the fact that you are naturally plan oriented and determined, and see through that to deal with things at home. Your spouse may or may not be on the same schedule as you, especially not when you throw in a few kids. Come home and instead of setting the tone and running the show following your perceived schedule, see what has been working during the time you've been gone and try to adapt to it. It's much easier for just you to adapt to their schedule than it is for all of them to adapt to yours. "Facts are stubborn things; and whatever may be our wishes, our inclinations, or the dictates of our passion, they cannot alter the state of facts and evidence," said John Adams.

Now What?

Up to this point in this chapter, we have been somewhat in control of situations or actions to deal with them. However, when find ourselves in situations where the control lies in the hands of others, we fight great battles against stress and anxiety, especially when things don't go according to plan. We operate by a set of rules and regulations, we know when to do certain things on the job and have expectations from others involved in the operation. When things don't go as planned, we adapt and seek the next best solution. For those of you reading this book that commute to work or plan on commuting, this is a huge issue you are dealing with or are about to deal with.

When you plan your commute to work, you are relying on external factors to align in order for you to get to work. Even if you are lucky enough to have a single flight to get to your base, you are still relying on the weather, the crew, the schedule, and then hope the plane doesn't break. Any one of these things could throw a wrench into your wheel and force you to come up with a new plan in a matter of minutes.

I can't tell you how many times I have been at the gate of a flight going to work and some type of delay occurs. Then you have to think about switching to another flight, or maybe waiting for the original one to go after all. Immediately anxiety takes over and you start to think of all the things that could go wrong. What if you switch to a different flight and that one is delayed as well, meanwhile your original flight takes off. We are used to controlling situations and running the show, but when we put the fate of circumstances in the hands of others, we are subject to great anxiety when things begin to fall apart.

This feeling of anxiety, over years, will have detrimental health affects, something we seldom place enough value on over the span of our careers. It would be interesting to see a study on how long a commuter versus a person that lives in his or her base lives after retiring at age 60 or 65. I am willing to bet the results would make you think twice about commuting to work. I commute myself over 3,000 miles to work, I wouldn't want to know how many ulcers I have given myself stressing about getting to work or home. We all need to keep the ultimate cost of stress in mind.

"Those who do not know how to fight worry die young."

Dr. Alexis Carrel

CHAPTER 13
Everything Has Its Costs

"Anything that just costs money is cheap."
John Steinbeck

Sam grew up in Arizona and spent his childhood years staring up at the sky and dreaming about being a bird. His dad was a naval aviator in the war, so the "flying bug" ran in the family. He used to ride his bike to the small executive airport, which was about eight miles from his home; he would solo before he would drive a car by himself. Every weekend he would ride his bike out to the airport and listen to the ground school instructors give their lessons to their students during all various phases of their fight training. The flight instructors were impressed by his passion and dedication, so they took it upon themselves to always make sure he would be included where possible.

Eventually, Sam built up the nerve to ask the flight students if he could sit in the back of the planes during training flights, which most had no problem with. Sam recalls the worst lessons to sit in the back of, were the ones where they did stalls and steep turns. A hot summer day in Arizona, low altitude, and then floating weightlessly over and over again while

142

practicing stalls. Then as if that wasn't enough, another 30-minutes of steep turning, pushing Sam's stomach to his feet, all while sweating like a dog in a Chinese restaurant (just kidding, kind of). But it's amazing how much you learn from sitting in the back seat watching, often times recognizing mistakes before they happen because you saw them happen so many times before. So when the time came for Sam to do his flight training, he was very well versed and proficient, even after just completing the minimum hourly requirements. He earned his ratings at all the age limitations, and before you knew it he was in the right seat of a regional airliner at age 20. His dreams were fulfilled; he did it, like-father-like-son. He was making $14/hr. (70 hours per month), which to him was a fortune. Jumpseating around the country on days off, he simply couldn't get enough of it.

Michelle was a very attractive young woman growing up in Lincoln, Nebraska. She grew up in a wealthy family, however, her parents divorced when she was still a young girl. She had two older sisters that both, like their father, went into the medical field and became doctors. She was the only non-doctor in the family and often times felt that she was disappointing her dad for going against the family trade. She did however love the idea of interacting with people and selling products, and since she was so familiar in the medical field, she chose to sell medical equipment for a large company. Her bond with her mom was very strong as the older sisters bonded more with their father, perhaps because they were more like him professionally. Her mom just wanted Michelle to be happy, so if being in sales was it, then so be it. Michelle was hired right out of college by one of the largest medical companies in the world and was to sell products all over the country. The job was challenging yet rewarding. She spent almost all week on the road, which she really enjoyed since she loved to travel.

THE TERMINAL

Sam can still remember the day like it was yesterday. He checked in at the ticket counter for his usual commute to work. The flight was fairly full but he felt somewhat confident that he would make it on the flight. Hungry for breakfast, he walked down the terminal to a fast food vendor, grabbed a coffee and donut, found a nice quiet spot near his gate, and sat down. He was sipping his coffee, staring over at the news streaming on the airport TV monitors, when he suddenly caught the glimpse of a young blond woman, very attractive and dressed professionally, sitting across the walkway from him. Their eyes met and she offered a very subtle smile, then focused on typing away on her phone.

Sam remembers thinking that something clicked inside of him that moment their eyes met, but not thinking anymore of it. Boarding began and the young woman got up and walked to the gate. Traveling as a standby passenger, you typically board last, so Sam waited until boarding was complete and standby passengers were called. He received one of the last empty seats and proceeded to walk down the jet way. He peeked in the cockpit to introduce himself and thank the crew for a ride, then walked down the aisle toward his seat row. About half way down, just behind the exit row, he found his assigned seat, a middle seat, and Sam couldn't believe who was sitting right next to him by the window. The same blond woman he saw in the terminal was now right next to him, what a coincidence he thought. The flight departed and Sam sat quietly, trying to think of what, and if, he should say anything to her at all. Out of the corner of his eye, he could see that she was typing on her laptop so he figured it best not to disturb her. About an hour into the flight, she excused herself to use the restroom. Sam got up to let her out and when she returned he took the opportunity to say hello. He asked where she was going, where she worked, and the next thing he knew they were lost in a wonderful conversation. Time flew by, and a long flight suddenly became not long enough for the two.

"CALL ME"

Time had flown by for both of them, both equally enjoying their conversation and hearing each other's stories. Sam considered himself slightly shy but after they landed he told her how much he enjoyed talking to her and wished her well. The plane arrived at the gate and everyone got off, including her. Again, typically as a standby passenger, you board last and also deplane last. So Sam watched his seatmate leave and he waited for the rest of the plane to deplane, grabbed his bags and walked off the plane himself. As he walked off the jet bridge into the terminal, he was shocked to see the woman standing there looking right at him as if she had been waiting for him. She approached Sam and told him that she really enjoyed talking with him, and gave him her number to call if he ever found himself in her neck of the woods. Sam played it off as cool as he could, but it took all he had to not skip and whistle down the terminal with joy. He went to work, never once able to stop thinking about her. He kept looking at the paper that her number was on, her name, Michelle, written right below it. Unbeknown to both, their relationship had just started; little did they know what crazy road lay ahead.

Sam called Michelle the very next day and they spent hours on the phone. Day after day, they spent hours talking to each other. Although she travelled a lot during the week, Sam began to fly to the cities where she was working on his days off. Soon they would see each other a few days a week regularly. Then on her days off, instead of flying home, she would go meet Sam, often in a mutually decided city they both loved to visit and spend a few romantic days together. Napa, Vegas, L.A., Miami, Hawaii, you name it, they had a blast and their relationship really blossomed. They both did exactly what they loved for work, and then on days off could go anywhere they wanted to, Sam for free and usually in first class; Michelle had so many miles she could pretty much do the same. Sam knew the next step in their relationship was to propose, so he saved for a few months and bought a beautiful diamond ring. They had traveled to Hawaii before and on the next trip out there he decided he would propose. They both enjoyed the outdoors and bike riding, so the setup was perfect. While visiting Maui during their next trip on days off, they took a van ride up to the Haleakala Volcano early in the morning before sunrise. They would watch the sun rise out of the ocean, and then ride bikes back down the volcano. The lack of sunlight and high altitude on top made it freezing cold. So here they were, bundled up in a cozy blanket, sitting on top of a volcano. The horizon turned purple, then orange, becoming brighter every minute. Right when the first glimpse of the sun rose up above the horizon, he asked Michelle to marry him. A new sun, a new life, together.

CLIPPING YOUR WINGS

Once engaged, Sam decided that since he could commute from anywhere to work, they would share an apartment near her company's headquarters. Michelle had been very successful at her job and received several promotions during the time she had dated Sam. Promotions also meant more supervising and managing her sales team, so she began to travel less and spent more time in the office. When she did travel, her trips now took her all over the world. Their lives became more hectic, trying to balance their work schedules and still wanting to travel, often times weeks would pass before they had the same days off together.

Sam was still focused on working for an international airline and spent a lot of time updating his applications. Then finally one day, Sam received a phone call inviting him to interview for a pilot slot at a major international airline. However, the airline was based in Seoul, South Korea. He figured he didn't have much of chance considering that he is flying a plane now about the size of the airline's smallest airplane's engine, so why would they hire him? The interview went terrible and he felt very intimidated by the other applicants interviewing that day. But to his total surprise, they offered him the job; class would begin in four months.

Sam and Michelle now had some serious soul searching to do. Taking the job would mean having to be in training for six months without having the opportunity to come home, she would rarely ever have enough days off to make the long trip to see him. Michelle respected his dreams of flying a big jet all over the world, so she encouraged him to take the job and they would figure out how to see each other somehow, after all it was only six months of their lives. Sam had mixed emotions, excited to start his new job, yet sad to leave his life the way he knew it and loved so much. Training went well, although very stressful, he finished and six months went by quickly. Michelle managed to come out twice to see him, the rest of the time she stayed very busy at work figuring the busier she was, the faster time would pass. Sam was finally living his dream, flying to exotic destinations all over the globe. Michelle was happy for Sam but started to miss the lifestyle they once lived so perfectly. She missed the excitement of experiencing new places, staying at new hotels and enjoying nice meals and cocktails into the late hours with Sam. With that being said, deep down she always wanted to become very successful at her job, if nothing else just to prove to her dad that she could do it. As much as she missed their old life, she loved her job and the challenges it came with. As with every challenge, there was a reward consisting of promotions or some form of acknowledgment for her hard work.

BABY FEVER

For Sam, flying long haul meant that his trips were usually longer in length but the stretches of days off were longer as well. Michelle's friends were now busy with raising their kids and instead of meeting for coffee in the afternoon followed by a nice bi-weekly girls night out dinner and wine, they would have to chauffeur the kids around to sporting events or take care of their babies. Michelle loved her job more than anything, besides Sam of course, but she felt that there was one thing missing from her life. Michelle and Sam had talked about kids, both always said they wanted children but had been so busy that it never was a real issue, until now. Michelle caught the bug; she wanted to have kids of her own now. Sam was hesitant at first but warmed up to the idea of being a dad. After a few romantic getaways, Michelle was pregnant with their first child. The company she worked for offered great maternity leave so Michelle planned on taking the maximum time off with the baby.

Michelle was a little more than nine months pregnant when Sam was setting out for his last long trip before he would stay home until after the birth. Sam landed just about half way around the world from their home when he got a message to call home. Michelle was panicked, she was having cramps and didn't know if she was going into labor or just having false contractions. She felt so stressed as there was still a thousand things she felt needed to be done before their son was born, not to mention that Sam wasn't home.

Funny how that works out, you have almost ten months to plan and prepare, but no matter how much you accomplish in that time there still seems to be more to do. I am that way myself with packing for a trip. I will be home for a week and know exactly when I have to leave for my next trip. The week goes by and then suddenly it's 30 minutes before I have to walk out the door, nothing packed, dirty uniform shirt, still need to shower, complete madness.

Anyway, so Sam is now equally panicked because he doesn't want to miss the birth of his first son, and hearing the stressed voice of his wife didn't help matters. This was the first time in his life that he actually questioned his career choice. Up to this point in his life, he loved every part of his job. But now suddenly, all he wanted to do was be home. His love for his dream job that he worked so hard for all his life now was in question.

So Close Yet So Far Away

Everything has a price; sometimes we don't realize that until much later in life. Missing the birth of your first child is a pretty high price to pay, something that Sam never had to think about until now. What about birthdays, holidays, first steps, sporting events, the list goes on. You basically miss half of your life at home; the thought of all of this was overwhelming to Sam. He felt like his whole world was crumbling in front of him, his stomach tensed up and he felt nauseous. He immediately contacted crew scheduling and explained the situation, they were very supportive and arranged a ticket home right away. From South Korea back home was a long way, and Michelle would have to hold off giving birth to their son for at least 20 hours. But that was the best Sam could do considering the circumstances. He was so tired from spending all day in an airplane flying to Seoul, and now he had to turn around and head right back. His mind was filled with so many different emotions, thoughts and feelings he never felt before. Why did he go on this one last trip? Maybe he should have stayed home earlier? Why did he have to fly for an airline that takes him so far from home? What kind of father would he be, will his son be mad when he goes to work for a week at a time or more?

Sam landed at home after being awake for nearly 40 hours, felt too tired to drive and got in a cab. Michelle had gone to the hospital the night before and was in full force labor. She gave birth to their beautiful healthy baby boy 20 minutes before Sam walked into the birthing room. Sam remembers crying like a baby when he saw Michelle holding their son in her arms. Joy, love, fear, anger, fatigue, were just some of the feelings that rushed through his head. Michelle pretty much felt the same but was glad that Sam was there now, she didn't have to be alone anymore. Two days later the three of them drove home and started their new life together, just with much less sleep now with the baby.

WHO WILL STAY HOME WITH THE KIDS?

Michelle had another few months of maternity leave but Sam was due to go back to work in two weeks. They sat on their couch one night after the baby went to sleep, and for the first time the reality of raising a child while both having careers hit them. Michelle's job was starting to change a little during this time. Corporate layoffs meant that her team had shrunk significantly. As a result, she would have to do a lot of the traveling herself now. Who would stay home with the baby? Could they coordinate their schedules opposite, so that one would go to work while the other would stay home. When would they ever see each other this way? What about if they hired a nanny? Maybe one of them should quit and stay home full time with their son? Both of them had worked so hard all their life to land the job that they both had now, how could they decide who would quit.

Sam's first trip after the birth quickly approached, and for the first time in his life, he was dreading it. He never thought he would ever dread going to fly an airplane across the world, but he was. What was the cost of this trip he thought to himself, what will I miss this time? He still was angry for missing the birth, especially because he was so close to making it, what was going to happen next. The true cost of his career was now a factor; his dream job was suddenly an obstacle in spending time with the most precious gift in life, his child.

Michelle was not much support this time because for one she was giving up her dream job for the time being, but secondly he was going to do what he loved and get good sleep in a hotel while she was up every hour of the night feeding their newborn. The process of giving birth and having a newborn is obviously an incredible undertaking for the mother, so needless to say

Michelle was quite stressed and emotionally drained. Their new lifestyle became a task, one that instead of being filled with new adventures and exciting new destinations, was now managing sleep and feeding schedules. When Sam would go to work, he would terribly miss seeing his son every day and being there to support his wife. Michelle was left alone, exhausted and the fact that Sam was back to what he was doing before didn't make her feel any better. Even though she knew the stress and challenges the job entailed, she was so exhausted and tired that she was envious of Sam getting more than three straight hours of sleep.

This went on for about five months and now it was time for Michelle to start thinking about going back to work. The thought of leaving her baby broke her heart, something she never thought about before. Now for the first time in her life, she looked at her dream job from a different perspective. Her dream job now meant not seeing her baby, something that is not easily overcome. Not to mention, the cost of her going back to work was not only not seeing her son, but also meant not seeing Sam since they would need to travel on opposite schedules to ensure one of them was at home. So after long deliberations and discussions, they mutually decided that it's best for their family to have Michelle resign from her job and focus on raising their child. Although the decision was difficult for Michelle, the thought of leaving her son was not something she was willing to accept.

Over the next few months, Sam had gotten used to being gone for a week or two, seeing his son mostly on the computer which was fun and made him feel more connected to home.

Distances seemed to shrink and there was hardly a day when he didn't get to see his child even if just via the computer. Michelle had recovered well from giving birth and now they felt ready to expand their family further. Before they knew it, baby number two was on the way and they were very excited for their new addition. This time Sam made sure he was home plenty of time ahead of the due date and was able to greet his second son as he was born. Another two years later, their third child was born and they now had a wonderful healthy little family. When Sam returned from his trips he would try to relieve Michelle of as many duties as he could to give her a much-deserved break.

MISSING THE GOOD TIMES BUT FORGETTING THE BAD

You ever think back to an ex relationship and find yourself missing certain aspects of it? It seems like when we do this, we think of the positive things in the relationship and disregard the negatives. This makes you think that perhaps it wasn't all that bad after all and you start to view the time as a positive experience. It's not until you deliberately force yourself to think about all the headache and drama that caused you to break up in the first place, that you realize what a nightmare you had escaped. Ernessa T. Carter wrote in her book, *32 Candles*, "That's the thing people never warn you about with breakups. It's the good times that really get you. In fact, they hurt worse than the bad times."

The same goes with old jobs sometimes and in Michelle's case she started to think just that. She would think back to her days traveling all around the world to exotic places, having nice dinners with colleagues and clients, then waking up the next morning after a good night's rest, to fly to the next destination to do it all over again. What she wasn't thinking about was the fatigue and how tired you felt after a weeklong trip around the globe. You would be up all night, trying to catch up on sleep during the day, eating strange foods at weird times, then fighting jet leg while pitching a multi-million dollar sales deal to clients. Sam would come home after such a trip and be exhausted to no end, having been up for more than 24-hours just to make it home as quickly as possible and then jump right into the daily family routine. He said often he would start his day in South Korea, fly all night, all day, and then all night again to make it home right about the time the kids woke up. Then it was a quick shower to get the airplane smell off and the day would begin new. Michelle was ready for a break and would go out and meet her friends for coffee in peace and quiet. Sam would play with the kids and try to stay awake during their naps to catch up on the mail and bills that have piled up while he was away. After dinner he would give the kids a bath and then put them to sleep, jumping into bed himself right after for the first time in over two days.

3 A.M.

Then one of two things usually happens, and for those of you reading this that have international flying experience, you will understand this well. You either wake up at 3 a.m., wide awake, with a headache because you haven't had coffee in a while, or you would sleep all night because you were so overtired and then the second night would wake up at 3 a.m., wide awake. You walk around the house in the early hours and finish opening the mail, pay some more bills, then right about the time when you feel you could go back to bed the first kid wakes up and is ready to play trains and fire trucks. The good news is that it does get better each night, but when you finally are adjusted back to a normal sleep schedule, it's time to go back to work and do it all over. But again, Michelle was thinking back to the good parts of that, the sleeping in hotels and having dinner without having the kids crawl under the table playing "eat off the floor" with their siblings. She envied Sam and his job, and this envy grew and grew.

My Turn

A few years went by and the youngest boy was about three, when Michelle started to crack some sales strategy books refreshing her memory. She wanted to go back to selling and traveling. She missed it so much and figured that since she had been at home for the past few years, it was Sam's turn now. The kids were old enough to not need mommy at home every day and so she could just go back to her old company and start back at the bottom. This of course meant even worse pay and quality of life, terrible schedules and having to travel to the cities where the managers didn't want to go to themselves. Sam was making good money, had gained good seniority at his airline and was able to pay the bills without having her work. On top of that, as much as Sam hated being gone from home, he loved his job and the schedules simply became part of their life. Now Michelle wanted him to quit his job, start at the bottom again, and work for a company making barely enough money to feed her, let alone the entire family. Needless to say, this created many long nights filled with emotional talks and sometimes even shouting matches, usually ending in tears and nothing being resolved.

One can see how this was a difficult issue with Sam and Michelle, both being madly in love with each other, yet also sharing that same love with their jobs. Having kids is something that changes just about every aspect of your life. Having two parents working full time is one thing, but having two parents working full time at jobs that take you away from home is another. Some couples are fortunate enough to have family nearby so that they have support while away from home, but the only other alternative is to have a nanny with the kids. Sam and Michelle had discussed this option of hiring a full time nanny, but they both decided that they didn't want someone else raising their children, and so that option was ruled out. Michelle had worked so hard to get the job of her dreams and therefore knew in her heart that she could always accomplish anything she set out to do. But this was different. Part of her knew that her plan to go back to work was not really financially feasible, but the thought of not doing what she had worked so hard for was also weighing on her. Then, of course, there was the idea of not being able to see her kids every day. However, she saw how Sam successfully balanced both worlds, so she felt confident that she could do the same.

So now it was decision time, what would they do now? Would she go back to work and Sam could stay home with the kids? They could live off of their savings to supplement the lost income and then hopefully by the time that ran dry, she would have been able to move up to a management position or a better paying job. Suddenly, she was hit again with the realization that the true cost of traveling for a living is high, much more than she ever imagined it being. She would be gone from her kids half of their lives, they would eat through years worth of savings, Sam would walk away from years' worth of longevity at his current job, and all of this with hopes that she can land a better job by the time the savings were gone. Worst case, maybe she could cash in some of the kids' college funds, maybe even tap into their retirement account. Holy cow, all of this to get to work a traveling job?

WHEN BOTH PARENTS WORK FULL-TIME

Sam and Michelle's situation is not uncommon among couples where both are working professionally and both love their careers. Both have worked hard to get to where they are so the thought of quitting that job is difficult for many. When you introduce children to a relationship, you are opening a new full time position that is guaranteed to be much more challenging than any job in the world. Some take this job on full time, others rather not or cannot afford to. If it's financially not feasible to have one stay home then both parents work, but either way one of them is home with the kids every night. This opens the option of day care at least, something not possible when both parents are away from home overnight. When one partner quits their job to assume a much more difficult and challenging one, issues naturally arise.

Michelle would often ask Sam if he had a nice vacation with his buddies, or if he needed more sunscreen for his next trip, but she only did that because she was jealous that he was still traveling and she was stuck at home. For Sam, this made it even harder to be gone from home because he didn't feel appreciated. It is therefore vital in any relationship that appreciation is given where due, often times such a simple thing is easily overlooked and will grow into a much greater issue down the road. Sam is working hard to provide for his family; Michelle is working even harder to raise the children at home. Both are working hard and both deserve appreciation from the other. A simple "Honey, I am so thankful to have you at home with our children and doing such an amazing job raising them, especially when I am gone so much." Or her saying, "Honey, I know it's difficult being away from home but I appreciate you working hard to support our family." Both are so simple and actually go much further than you would think, especially if said at times when those words can really mean the world to the other person.

FEEDBACK

Parenthood is a job where initially there is no acknowledgment from the kids. When they are little, they eat, poop, and sleep, not necessarily in that order. There is no feedback at all, zero. Then after a few months they begin to smile at you, your heart immediately fills with love and joy as you finally feel like there is feedback coming your way. That quickly fades when your friends tell you that these smiles are only gas smiles, meaning that they are not really smiling at you. You go back to square one but again after a few more months the smiles become sincere and you feel an incredible connection with your child. The point here is that Michelle always received acknowledgment from her previous employer for her hard work. She missed that, very much so indeed. She was now working harder than ever and felt frustrated that her work did not seem acknowledged or appreciated.

Michelle's envy of Sam's job grew more and more and eventually became pure resentment every time he went to work. The more resentment she felt, the more she would throw little jabs at Sam, which made him feel even more frustrated. The most dangerous part of this viscous cycle is your attitude towards your children. You never want them to feel that they are the reason, even though they unintentionally might be, that you are not happy staying at home. Michelle and Sam's relationship started to become more and more hostile; eventually they weren't even sleeping in the same bed anymore.

THE LIFE CHANGING CONFERENCE

Then one day, when Sam was home for a long stretch of days off, Michelle flew out to a sales seminar in Las Vegas. She was excited to be out and about again, she had been there many times before so knew all the good spots to visit. The meeting was great and really encouraged her to begin working again. She met lots of very successful sales people from all different fields. The last night the main speaker was a very known and well-respected sales manager in the medical field. Michelle had met her before at a convention a few years back in Chicago, so she was eager to hear her speak. After her presentation, the speaker walked down and shook hands with people that had gathered to hear her speak. Michelle figured this was a great time to say hello again and so she made her way towards the speaker. She introduced herself and the lady immediately remembered Michelle from their previous encounter. Michelle was pleasantly surprised that she had been remembered, she was more known among her colleagues than she had thought. The lady invited Michelle for a drink at the bar in the hotel where the convention was taking place.

Both hit it off beautifully and they shared great stories. Toward the end of the night, the lady told Michelle that she loved her career dearly, however had one regret. That regret was not spending as much time as possible with her two kids when they were younger. Right then, Michelle had a light bulb go off in her head. In the grand scheme of things, your kids are only little for a brief period in your life. You have such a small window of opportunity to be with them and touch their lives. The time you spend with them during such an influential period will shape their minds to what kind of person they will grow to become. So many families do not have an opportunity to spend so much time with their kids, but Michelle had it. A chance many would die for, to be able to raise your own children while they were still at home every day. Soon enough, they would be in school and playing sports, your time with them will go from all the time to hardly at all. The lady told her to enjoy each day with them, they are precious times, and before she knows it the kids would be grown. Selling will always be there, your kid's childhood won't. Michelle thanked her for her time and lovely conversation; little did the lady know that she just changed a person's life forever. The next day Michelle flew back home, her life truly changed.

A NEW OUTLOOK

Sam noticed right when he first saw Michelle that something had changed. A heavy burden seemed to have been lifted. She was filled with joy and life, smiled again and was a joy to be around. Her relationship with Sam went back to being the way it was before this period began, perhaps even better. A few years became 10 years, and she still is enjoying raising her kids and driving them between sporting events. She had thought about going back to work full time, but now the thought of just traveling to places she wanted to go to with Sam was more enticing than traveling there for work. The kids would be out of the house soon, then when Sam had days off they could travel to wherever they wanted to, just like they did when they first met. Today they are both happily married, Sam is a senior Captain and they both love to travel on his off days. The kids are all in college, have a great relationship with their parents, and look back on their childhood with fond memories. With that being said, none of them want to work in the traveling industry or medical field.

Opportunity costs can be significant and most costs are not measurable by numbers. What's it worth to miss your first child's birth? What about missing their first steps, words, home run at T-ball, Christmas Eve with the family at home…. the list is endless. There is no money value to this, but a value each one of us places individually on them. As bad as that sounds, there are equally as many positives that come with this job. How many parents can take their kids to school and pick them up again every day? What about taking a vacation in the middle of the week when everyone else is at work? You and your family also get used to the lifestyle and adapt to it. When your children are young, they are more concerned about what present Santa brought them than if they get to open it the 25th or on the 29th. You can move birthdays, Easter, Thanksgiving, anything really. Then when the kids get a little older they can have multiple celebrations, one with their friends perhaps, and the other when both parents are home. What kid doesn't want to celebrate their birthday twice a year?

The biggest challenge we face overall is our own emotions and ourselves. Us being away from home and missing certain events from our lives is harder on us than it is on the kids, this is even truer with little kids. My three year old misses me for about a day or two, and then is busy worrying about finding candy and chasing squirrels in the park. If I get home at noon or at 4 p.m., he doesn't know the difference. Those four hours are huge for us and can change the entire commute home based on connection times, etc. So we place this stress upon ourselves and once we realize this concept we can try to look at it differently. Your family and the kids will survive whether you get home on Monday morning or Monday night, but you might not for long, if you give yourself ulcers stressing about getting home. Everything has its cost, you have to decide on your own what you are willing to pay to live the lifestyle that you wish to live.

CHAPTER 14
Embrace Technology

"The speed of communications is wondrous to behold. It is also true that speed can multiply the distribution of information that we know to be untrue."

Edward R. Murrow

Back in the days before high-tech computers and the Internet, when you went on an international trip, you might have been out of touch for days, if not weeks at a time. You could literally live separate lives and get away with it. That reminds me of a funny story, for us reading at least. A guy, let's call him John, was an international pilot and loved to have just a little too much fun on his overnights. He was married, three children under the age of 12 and lived in a nice home in a big city. His marriage was dull; he seemed content but not too thrilled to be in this relationship. Over the years of marriage, they drifted apart and became functioning roommates. The romance was almost seasonal it was so rare, but nevertheless his wife had been faithful for all those years. Life was extremely busy at home for them with their kids, at the end of the day very little time was left and it was considered a treat to take a long hot shower without having one of the kids walk in.

PHOTOSTREAM

John defined having a good time as a little more than the average guy would, often times taking him to shady bar scenes and not necessarily coming back to the hotel alone. He also loved taking pictures of his good times, and the more he drank, the more pictures he seemed to take. Well one day, while at home, he took a field trip to his local electronics store looking for a new toy. He came home with a new Apple TV, which he would use to stream movies at home and listen to music. It was also great because he could view pictures on the big screen TV and show his family. He loved taking pictures not only of his party times, but also of the local sights he would explore while on the road. He always erased the bad pictures before coming home so figured he was covering all his tracks of his secret party life on the road. His phone also had a great feature called Photostream, which was nice because it would save lots of space on his phone. The photos would automatically upload once connected to the Internet; you didn't have to sync to save your photos on your computer anymore. Can you see where this is going yet?

What this guy didn't realize is that the screensaver for his brand new Apple TV was linked to his Photostream by default. So one early morning after he stumbled back to his hotel room, his phone connected to the Internet and the photos, many of which were very inappropriate for any married man, were automatically streaming to the big screen TV at his home, halfway across the world, where his wife and kids were enjoying family time. Needless to say this didn't end well for this guy and not only did he have to explain things to his wife (soon to be ex-wife) but also his kids. Obviously John had other underlying issues in his life that lead to this disaster in the first place, but it goes to show you how vulnerable and instantaneous things are now days. We live in a world where privacy is virtually non-existent and you are potentially always being watched or tracked, usually we aren't even aware of it. Every week it seems like we learn about some hacking going on where thousands of identities with personal information are stolen or leaked, this will get much worse in years to come.

GOING TO WORK ON THE GOLF COURSE

There is another story that took place a while back. This individual was very old fashioned and refused to adapt or accept technology as it became available over the years. He had no cell phone, was computer illiterate, and loved to play golf. He would go to the country club on many of his days off and enjoy nine holes in the morning, a relaxing lunch, and then nine holes in the afternoon. He was married for over 35 years and their grown children were out of the house long ago. His wife spent most of her time painting and loved taking art classes at the local community college. One day, one of his children got into a car accident, nothing too major but still requiring a trip to the hospital. She wanted to call her husband but since he didn't carry a cell phone was unable to reach him. Desperately trying to get a hold of him, she called crew scheduling to have them contact her husband and let him know what had just happened. They were surprised to hear from her and politely informed her that her husband had retired over a year ago. So for over a year now, the husband would leave his house in his pilot uniform and suitcase, and go on a golfing vacation, often never leaving his hometown at all. He enjoyed the life style of being able to leave for a few days a month and was not willing to give it up. We get so used to our lifestyle that the very thought of a sudden change can leave us helpless and without purpose. The moral of the story here is to buy a cheap cell phone if you are going to do what this guy did. No, but all joking aside it just goes to show you how we are now living in a world where we are almost always contactable and traceable.

Texting And Cheating

Recently, I was talking with a colleague who had just gotten divorced. He was married for more than 15 years, no kids and his wife worked part time at a gym as a personal trainer. She had been acting rather standoffish over the past few months leading up to the separation and he was starting to have doubts over her doings while he was away on trips. He would usually be gone for periods of 8-10 days and then home for the same time he was gone. One evening they were cuddled up on the couch together catching up on their favorite TV shows they liked to watch, a nice glass of wine and some chocolate he had bought home from his last trip to Germany. She got up to use the restroom for a minute and her phone, which she had sitting next to her, vibrated signaling a text message. He glanced over and saw that it was a local number and it simply said: "alone?" Finding this rather strange, he looked at her incoming text messages and noticed that only very few text messages were on her history list, which seemed very strange since she was texting all the time throughout the day. Not thinking too much more about this he enjoyed another few days at home and then went back on the road.

While away, he discussed what had happened with another colleague and he had mentioned that you could download a program that lets you look at erased messages. He at first thought it was a silly idea, after all he trusted his wife. But then after giving it more thought, he figured at least by doing that he would not worry about it anymore and could put this behind him. He downloaded the program and was in total shock to see that she had been secretly texting and seeing multiple guys in town while he was away on trips. She had been romantically involved with one particular guy for more than a year. Needless to say when he returned from his trip, he confronted his wife and she basically confessed to all that he had found, after all how could she deny it? She used technology to communicate in secret, and he used that same technology to find out about it. If you think you are being secret about anything now days, you might want to think twice about that.

This technology can be the greatest tool for any traveling person. Distances shrink tremendously, and if you wanted to, you could see your family every day on the computer. Many people place a camera device or a computer on the dining table where they usually sit, and then when the family eats at night they can all see each other and have normal dinnertime conversations.

Bridging the Distance

I recently flew with a guy who spends several hours a day on the computer tutoring his kids with homework, just as if he was standing right next to them even though he is thousands of miles away. When you have little kids, they seem to change every day, at least now you witness that change. Back before all of this fancy technology, you would come home after being on the road for three weeks and barely recognize your kids standing before you. Calling home while on a trip required you to buy phone cards, dial a hundred numbers and even then, just maybe, you would have a good enough connection to understand the person on the other end. Today we can call home and sound like we are across the street, streaming live video and even show everyone where we are. You can walk around New York City and your family on the west coast could watch you on their computer or phone as you take them sightseeing with you. It's incredible how much difference a quick video chat can make with loved ones; it re-energizes your soul and heart, both for you and for them. You can tell your kids a bedtime story and tuck them into bed in Florida, all while you are eating white rice with chicken in a local food stall in Singapore (they have Wi-Fi in the entire city, incredible).

Truly amazing if you think about how far technology has come and how much it has helped us in the travel industry stay connected with home. Embrace communication technology as it becomes available and utilize it to its fullest to bridge the gap between you and your family while you are on the road.

> *"Technological progress has merely provided us with more efficient means for going backwards."*
>
> *Aldous Huxley*

CHAPTER 15
Who Are You?

"Everyone thinks of changing the world,
but no one thinks of changing himself."

Leo Tolstoy

If you ask anyone who just went through a bitter divorce if they would have ever thought their marriage would end like it did, most would say not in a million years. Some couples drift apart, realizing that they are better off separated and part on somewhat good terms. But for the most part, they usually end up really strongly disliking each other. I have heard many hate stories about ex husbands or wives, most make you wonder how they could have ever gotten along in the first place. "My husband and I have never considered divorce... murder sometimes, but never divorce," said Joyce Brothers.

PIRATES OF THE CARIBBEAN

One extreme case I remember was one where the husband hated his ex wife so much, the very thought of paying her any alimony killed him. Working for a foreign airline, the rules of seniority were much different than we are accustomed to here in the United States. He actually decided to kill himself on paper, figuring then his ex wife would get no alimony since he no longer existed. He then thought of a new name to go by, he would continue working for the airline under this new name. What could possibly be a good name for an airline Captain that was untraceable? One that when searched for, would lead to anyone but him? Well say hello to Captain Jack Sparrow, also known as the fierce pirate in the Disney films. No kidding, that was his new name and I guarantee if you try to look up his name you would find a million pictures of Jonny Depp, but never this Captain himself.

MAKING IT AS INCONVENIENT AS POSSIBLE

I've heard of bitter wives calling the company which their ex's work for and falsely claiming drug or alcohol abuse, just so that the ex spouse would have to take numerous unnecessary drug and alcohol tests. Some guys have called random pawn shops at shady regions to give them their ex partners social and birth date, inviting them to use the data freely.

During a recent interview, a guy was getting married to his second wife over on the coast of Italy. It was going to be a beautiful ceremony with close friends and relatives invited. The guy was married previously and had a 12-year-old daughter. She flew over to Italy with him to be at the wedding of course and the ceremony began right when the sun was going down. The wedding was perfect up to that point, right up to the time the bride walked down the aisle. The ex wife had bought herself a first class ticket to Italy, then hired a private car to take her to the wedding site. Then once she got there, she demanded to have her court appointed time with her daughter, I guess she had a right to see her two hours per week when she was with him. So of course, intentionally, she timed it right when the bride was walking down the aisle, and the entire wedding ceremony had to go on hold for two hours so that the daughter wouldn't miss it. To top things off, after they all got back to the states, the ex wife sent the guy a bill for the $13,000 it had cost her to fly to Italy and see her daughter, claiming that since he took her so far away from her, she had no choice but to spend that kind of money and he should have to pay for it. Of course the judge laughed at this ridiculous request but, nonetheless, he had to spend a few thousand dollars to defend himself, not to mention the delay in the middle of his ceremony.

FROM LOVE TO HATE

I ask myself how two people, who at one point in their lives, decided to love each other forever, can end up hating each other so much? How can relationships go from such bliss to such hatred, often times in very short periods of time? More importantly, are there signs which we just all fail to recognize?

When we first fall in love we are typically blind to the realities of the circumstances. We ignore the bad, and simply magnify the positives to block the negatives from being visible. Usually your friends will be able to see them since they are not subject to the "new love blindness," but you typically ignore their observations and comments. I have personally been to weddings which I know would not end well, and unfortunately, so far at least, I have been right every time. But still, why do these marriages end on such bad terms and often, with great hatred?

In today's society, we are victims of our own political correctness. The judicial system is very corrupt and old fashioned in some ways, yet modern in others. Some laws and customs are simply outdated as society has changed, yet the laws still apply to the old ways. An example is our divorce laws. They were written back in days where typically the man would provide for the woman and the woman would be the homemaker. In the rare occasion that marriages ended in a divorce, the wife needed alimony to be able to support herself, since she did not have a career of her own. Today, the workforce has changed completely and often times the financial and family roles are opposite from the way it was back then. Today, women are just as successful as men in the workforce and have equal earning potential. However when it comes to divorce laws, they are very much catering to the old ways of life. There are differences from state to state but nonetheless, the man typically will pay a significant amount of alimony for a long period of time. I know that most of the guys I fly with that are divorced pay more than 50 percent of their income to their ex wives, often until they retire. One guy told me once that a general rule of thumb is that you typically pay 50 percent of your income, for however many years you were married, plus half of all your assets. Often their ex wives would meet another man and even get engaged, but never marry since that would terminate the alimony payments.

Some countries now have adapted to new rules, which seem to level the playing field a little. The courts will look at the education the wife has received and what she has studied to do professionally. Then they take the average income that person would make and give her time to get spooled up with the profession. After such time she is expected to get a job in that field and her alimony payments will reflect that amount deducted from what the guy has to pay her. Of course this is all assuming that there are no dependent children involved and so on, every case is different but you get the general idea.

So the man is angry because he is basically giving half of his income to someone he doesn't even like anymore. At the same time, depending on what caused the divorce in the first place, the woman has various reasons for being angry with the guy, be it an affair or what have you. Either way, both partners really dislike each other for their own justified reasons. Please don't take this the wrong way, I do believe that certain situations call for certain settlements, but some of the stories you hear about are just plain crazy.

"WILL YOU MARRY ME, AGAIN?"

A good ending to an unfortunate one was a guy that divorced his wife over a girlfriend he had for more than a year. They had been married for more than 15 years, but the marriage had become dull and dry. No passion, no romance, no connection other than being good friends living under the same roof. This went on for more than five years, during which time he met a gal and started dating her. His new relationship was exciting and thrilling, something he knew was so wrong. Yet that seemed to make it even more exciting. He ended up leaving his wife for his girlfriend, got divorced, and started his new life with his new love. His divorce was not hostile, and both agreed that they had simply become friends and would be better off separate. The exciting and lust filled new relationship quickly turned into a regular one, where he felt that he was basically right where he was with his ex wife. Suddenly he realized that his affair had turned into a false illusion of a better life, something that he could now see right through. He broke up with his girlfriend, moved into a small apartment, and was determined to try to rekindle the love with his ex wife. They sat down together and discussed the various aspects of their 15-year marriage, identifying where things went wrong. They both vowed to ensure that those would not happen again and they ended up marrying again and lived happy ever after (at least so far).

Bottom line, we all tend to get complacent and lazy in our own relationships. Once you feel disconnect from your spouse, it's easy to get misled by feelings that you, at that moment, think will result in a happier life. Then down the road, you discover that you are right back to where you started from before. Often times it is not the spouse that needs to be replaced or fixed, it's you. If you realize that you are the one that needs to make a change or an effort to enrich your relationship, then that can be done much easier than the alternative. Instead of focusing on what someone else can offer outside of the marriage, redirect that focus to what can be done inside of it.

I WANT MORE

A dear friend of mine that I mentioned earlier is flying over in Dubai. He is a genuinely nice guy who was always very faithful to his now ex wife. They were married for a short four years and had no children or assets other than what they had saved in retirement. They drew up a fair "do it yourself" divorce agreement, splitting everything in half but giving him the credit card debt, which he was ok with. They had the agreement notarized at the U.S. embassy and she returned back home to move on with her life. He was paying her the agreed amount of alimony for a year, which would buy her enough time to get on her feet and find a job. Upon returning home she started to hang around some friends that had also recently gone through divorces and seemed to be getting a lot more than she had gotten out of the divorce. She went to the courts and told them that she felt threatened to sign the divorce papers in the Middle East, and therefore wanted to void the signed agreement. (Are you kidding me, threatened to sign a divorce paper in Dubai, give me a break.) But the judge granted her wish and so the divorce process started all over again. Thousands were wasted on lawyers and courts, something completely unnecessary. To make matters worse, she not only wanted half of his income for four years, she also wanted half of his housing allowance. This seemed totally unfair since he needed that money to pay for the high cost of living in Dubai. So let's say for example he made $9,000 a month, $6,000 in income and another $3,000 in housing allowance. She wanted $4,500 a month for four years, leaving him with $4,500 but since he would spend $3,000 on housing he would be left with $1,500 a month to live. "Paying alimony is like feeding hay to a dead horse," Groucho Marx said. How could this be fair at all? Well without going into it much further and venturing off topic, they ended up settling for an amount somewhere in the middle, but still, was enough to actually make my buddy consider quitting his job altogether so that he wouldn't have to pay her. Needless to say, you can imagine how my buddy felt about his ex wife. Nancy Astor said, "Sir, if you were my husband, I'd poison your tea." Winston Churchill said, "Madame, if you were my wife, I'd drink it!"

What has our society come to where this type of behavior is entertained in the courts? Bottom line is, you can easily see where the hatred stems from, and when children and custody issues get involved, the punching gloves really come off quickly. How is it that we can love someone so much, that we confess our love in front of all our family and friends at a wedding, and then later find ourselves to be so hateful toward that same person?

We have all heard these horror stories time after time again, but not until you experience this for yourself can you understand this love/hate phenomena. When your spouse, who you have shared your life with, turns against you, either through unfaithfulness or other things leading to a divorce, the realization of betrayal and disappointments changes the way you feel about that other person instantly, often times growing into hatred and resentment. The saddest part of this is when children are involved, for they often times get stuck right in the middle of those battles. Children are used as pawns in their parents' little games and that's just simply not fair. As a child, you try to believe everything your parents tell you. When one tells you that mommy is bad and the other tells you that daddy is bad, you become confused and don't know what to believe anymore. You should never have to take sides, but often times that is expected of you in order to please your parent and receive their love. If you are unfortunate enough to have to go through a divorce, at least keep your children in mind and try your best to keep them isolated from your adult battles. My oldest memory in life is one where both my parents were yelling at each other, not the best memory to have. Those experiences as a child get imprinted in your little head and stay with you forever.

ARGUING IN FRONT OF THE KIDS

Another thing to consider when you have children is how you argue in front of them. Conflict is a normal part of any healthy relationship, but making up is equally so. Clint Eastwood said, "They say all marriages are made in heaven, but so are thunder and lightning." So if you start to argue in front of your kids, then be sure to make up in front of them as well. That way they see that an argument can occur, but then afterwards leads to making up and getting along again. Many couples will start an argument, and then continue later on after the children go to bed. The children see the conflict start, but never experience the resolution. Then if the relationship ends up in a divorce, the children will be left with the notion that conflict leads to divorce, certainly not accurate and potentially scarring them for life.

I have a friend who thinks that every time he gets in a fight with his wife they are on the way to get divorced. So immediately when things get heated up, he retreats to protect himself and all communication shuts down. His mind starts to race thinking about all the things that will change once he is divorced, how their assets will be divided up, custody of the kids and so forth. All of this, because of a silly little fight with his wife, causing him completely unnecessary stress. His problems stem from his childhood, as his parents often fought in front of him and then eventually got divorced. They both remarried and the same exact thing happened again, both divorcing a second time each. So you can see how his current behavior stems from his past, something we should all keep in mind in our own lives.

> *"Educate your children to self-control, to the habit of holding passion and prejudice and evil tendencies subject to an upright and reasoning will, and you have done much to abolish misery from their future and crimes from society."*
>
> *Benjamin Franklin*

CHAPTER 16
Keeping It Fresh

"Romance leads to marriage, but love keeps the marriage alive."

Toni Sorenson

You wake up and find yourself absolutely freezing. You have the covers pulled all the way up to your head and still can't seem to get warm. You try to go back to sleep, but now notice that you have to go to the bathroom. You roll to the side of the bed, stand up, and then realize that all of the sudden you have no idea where the bathroom is. It's pitch dark in the room and now you can't even remember where the light switch is. For that matter, you don't even know where the nightstand is that had the light on it. In fact, now you realize that you have no idea where you are at all. You fumble around a bit and finally find the nightstand. You find the light and switch it on, but of course not without knocking over your water and phone off the receiver. You replace the handset, quickly looking for the name of the hotel and address on it so that you can remember where you are. Now it all quickly makes sense again, you go to the bathroom, adjust the room temperature and finally go back to bed.

Does this story sound familiar to you? For me personally, this happens about twice a year and never ceases to amaze me how confusing those few moments are where you are absolutely lost in your own hotel room. With that being said, the thought of coming home and sleeping in your own bed can be most enticing. Many of us spend at least half of the month on the road and eat at restaurants for every single meal of the day. A home cooked meal in your own kitchen sounds pretty good right about then. It's amazing how much you begin to miss things that you pretty much always took for granted before traveling so much, even down to your own toilet seat.

KEEP YOUR SUITCASE PACKED

Buck was a senior First Officer for a major airline based in Atlanta. He had been flying internationally for 10 years and usually bid to fly to Europe in the summer and Hawaii in the winter. Not a bad gig and his wife of 18 years and two kids lived comfortably in a nice house in Florida. To minimize his commutes, he backed his trips up as much as he could so was usually gone for 12 days in a row and then home for about 10. He would come home after his set of trips and be so glad to be sleeping in his own bed. His wife had been at home taking care of the kids and shuttling them back and forth to the various sporting events they were part of. She would do all the cooking for them, make sure all their homework was done and then take care of everything else in the household that needed to be taken care of. When Buck came home, all he could think about was a nice home cooked meal and a night in his own bed. His wife on the other hand, who had been home this whole time, was thinking about how nice it would be to go out to eat and have someone else do the cooking and dishes for a change. She loved traveling and loved to go to the beach for a few days with the family, a nice little getaway that would be a good break from the daily routine.

The last thing Buck wanted to do after being gone for 12 days was to pack his suitcase and stay in a hotel again. So herein lies the problem; the two both have justified wants that are opposite. His wife needed a break from being home; Buck needed a break from the hotels and just wanted to be home. When his wife would book a short getaway, Buck would get angry and made the entire trip not enjoyable for his family, since all he could think about was how he just wanted to be home. He knew that after coming home from the getaway, he would have to go back to work again, causing him to be stressed out all the time. His wife was angry and upset because she just wanted a break from the daily life she had while Buck was away on the road. After a few disastrous getaways, they agreed that his wife would invite her girlfriends instead to go on these little trips, and Buck would get to stay home with the kids and enjoy being home. This seemed to fix the problem temporarily; both got their own wishes. Since Buck was home with the kids, it was now easier for her to get away more. So her trips became more frequent and longer. Before they knew it Buck would return home just to see his wife in passing as she was out the door to set off on her little getaways.

This continued for about a year, when one day Buck noticed

she wasn't spending much money while away on her trips. Of course he wasn't complaining about that, but found it strange that she would be gone for 3 days and only have a small coffee shop charge and perhaps a gas station charge. Now he started to get more curious and started to do some recon work himself. He hired a private investigator to follow his wife on one of her little getaways and was shocked to learn that she was meeting up with another guy to travel with. Suddenly it all made sense, the guy was courting her so was picking up all the food tabs and incidentals which explained how she was getting away with not spending any money. He confronted her, and after confessing to him, they decided to split up. She fully blamed him for her affair and told him that if he had been more willing to travel with her, this would have never happened. She needed an escape from her daily life, and since he was never willing to do that she eventually found someone that would.

BALANCE

The moral of the story is that we need to recognize that balance is required in any healthy marriage. Of course we want to be home, but we need to remember that while we are away on the road, our spouses are home every day. At the same time, our spouses need to recognize that we have been traveling the entire time they were home, so we have a right to just want to be home. A balance is needed, one that is different for every relationship but nonetheless required. Determine what is important to the other person and try your best to make them feel that you respect that. It can be something as simple as a date night, or something extravagant like a quick weekend trip to Napa. Keep things fresh in your relationship; try to not get complacent, for that's when things often take a turn for the worse. It's easy to become roommates; each having set roles in the partnership that keeps things functioning but not being connected on a romantic level.

I have worked with guys that have been married for more than 20 years and consider themselves in a partnership with their spouses to raise their children. Once the kids move out of the house, they look at each other and realize that they have no romantic bond keeping them together and the marriage breaks apart. Some, however, use the opportunity to have a kid free house to actually reconnect and rekindle their romantic love life. They begin to travel and spend time together, rediscovering the very same elements that got them together in the first place. Keeping these same elements fresh in a marriage can be the determining factor between two people that reminds them of the reasons they are with them and will keep them together. Pay attention to your spouses needs and try to accommodate them in your lives, as for you that don't, there is always someone willing to do that for you. You each have an obligation to keep things alive in a relationship, but sometimes we are simply too lazy to put in the effort required. If you can take just part of your motivation you had to get to where you are today in your profession, you might be surprised to see how far that effort goes in your personal life.

"Love is that condition in which the happiness of another person is essential to your own."

Robert R. Heinlein

CHAPTER 17
Conclusion

"May your love and your relationship be modern enough to get you through each and every day, yet old fashioned enough to get you through a lifetime."

Unknown Author

I wish there was a secret recipe or a simple solution to a happy marriage in this industry, but unfortunately there is not one. Some marriages simply drift apart over time, some break apart due to affairs, but the one thing that they all have in common is how they began. All marriages start out in the "in love" phase, which seems to be endless at that time. Every wedding celebrates two individuals that have fallen madly in love and they can't imagine living a life without the other. Each feel that they truly know the other person and trust them with all that they have (literally). Some people simply change, becoming someone that they were not before. This happens to many and the transition seems to be very subtle, sometimes not noticeable until it's too late.

How many friends have you had that you used to really get along with and now you don't. This change can happen for countless reasons, for example a job change, money matters, children, or other big life changing events. For some, the change is manageable and can be turned into something positive, but for many, this is not the case. If you ask any divorcee if the person they initially married and the person they ended up divorcing appeared the same, the usually say no. The individual they married became someone that was completely different than before. If you can maintain awareness of the subtle changes, you might have the opportunity to either adapt or reshape that change into your lives to make it positive. The most important part of that is to realize that it's not only the other person that is changing, it is often times you yourself.

WILD RIDE

Our career is like riding a wild roller coaster. Things can go up and then quickly down again, all within a moments notice. Some of us find jobs that we have always dreamed of and life couldn't get any better. Then suddenly that job goes away and we find ourselves in uncharted territories. Our ability to adapt to situations is not only crucial for our daily jobs, but also for our relationships. Recognizing that things constantly change and evolve is a major step in our professional and personal lives. It is therefore equally important to find a spouse that is able to sustain such ups and downs throughout life. They will be tasked with being home alone, taking care of everything while you are gone. They must be able to take initiative and be strong enough to keep the family intact in your absence. Trust is a crucial element in the relationships we have while in this profession, never give reason for doubt, once that trust is gone it is extremely difficult, if not impossible, to ever get it back.

For those of you that have been flying for some time, you have heard your fair share of stories similar to the ones in this book. For those that are new to this job, you are about to hear a bunch of stories, so get ready and take notes. It's really just about learning from other people. Having the benefit of learning about so many different types of relationships, good and bad, is one of the best benefits of this job. It's almost like being a fly in a marriage counselor's office. You can hear all the stories and then learn from them. It really is a freebee, a chance to hear what works and what doesn't. Then apply those things you think might work for you to your own life and hopefully it works. Every person is different, just like every relationship is different, but the key elements are very much the same. To disregard the lessons learned by others would be throwing away a good opportunity to better your own life.

TAKE A LOOK IN THE MIRROR

Sometimes we need to take a look in the mirror and realize that the change does not always need to come from others, often times just you. It's always easier to change yourself than it is to change others. I have seen it time and time again; people get divorced and get remarried, just to find themselves in the same position as the first marriage. When you hear the details of these marriages, you realize that the only thing that changes is the other person's name. The fundamental issues that led to the failure were never addressed, like plugging a hole in the boat with your finger. While there might not be any water coming in, the hole is still there and eventually you will move your finger and sink. Not until you actually patch the hole will smooth sailing be ahead.

Being away from home, means that you are more likely to encounter tempting situations. I say this primarily because your accountability is not there as it is when you are home; it is easier to get away with things while gone. Technology has changed that significantly and we discussed some situations earlier where guys got themselves into trouble. But with that being said, it is always easier to avoid temptation in the first place than it is to deal with once faced by it. Love can blind you and lead you to do things you never thought possible, but always keep in mind that the eyeshades will eventually come off. We are so busy looking for greener grass that we sometimes forget to see the green grass we are standing on. You are with the spouse you are with for a reason; sometimes we lose sight of that reason and forget why we are with them at all. That's when things happen that you simply cannot undue. Therefore, it's important to think of the end result before beginning something you'll regret.

It's easy to become roommates with your spouse, I see that happen all the time. Of course you cannot keep that initial "in-love" phase going continuously, but a once in a while visit to that phase can really keep things fresh in a marriage. Try to never lose sight of the very reason you were attracted to the person you are with. Learn from others, have an open mind to their stories, take the good and try to apply it to your own life. Take the bad and try to avoid it, for there is no reason to make the same mistake someone sitting right next to you just made.

I hope this book finds you well and you have learned something while reading this. If nothing else, this book should encourage you to listen to stories and learn from them as much as possible. Times come and go, but the memories you make along the way will last a lifetime. Try to make those memories the best you possibly can, our time will eventually come to an end, you will then continue to live on in the memories of others. Make those memories beautiful ones for life is truly short. As I have said, the divorce rate in this country is more than 50 percent, closer to 70 percent in our industry and it's getting higher every year. We cannot change the past, but we can change the future. With the statistics in mind, knowing that every other pilot you meet is either divorced or will be in the near future, do everything you can to maintain a healthy relationship with your spouse. Talk to them, listen to them, and make sure you share common goals in life. You don't take a pilot's checkride without preparing for it, treat your marriage the same. Study, read, learn, listen about relationships, and try your best to take the good from every story and apply it in your own life.

MEMORIES

I want to leave you with a positive yet personal note. My grandfather recently passed away at age 92. He was the most remarkable man in the world and I considered him to be my best friend. He was happily married for more than 60 years. He was always humble, caring, loving, and thoughtful. He had a very successful business that he ran even up to a month before his passing, a sign of how much he loved it. When became ill and went to the hospital, the nurses and doctors could not believe how many people were there to support him. The hospital room was filled, chairs lined up in the hallway, flowers, balloons, you name it. They had never seen such a support network for anyone before; they were amazed. Shortly after he passed, all kinds of people started to appear with stories of how he touched their lives, some even 30 plus years ago. That's when I realized how important it is to live a good life and leave good memories. All the success he had at work, the Silver Star for his bravery on Iwo Jima, his purple heart, none of it mattered at the end of the day. What mattered was that he had so many people around him that truly loved him and whose lives he had touched over the years. The memories of him that live on in our hearts are far more valuable than anything you can physically buy or earn in life. For those memories will never fade away and will sustain time forever, passing from generation to generation, never losing its value.

"The life of the dead is placed on the memories of the living. The love you gave in life keeps people alive beyond their time. Anyone who was given love will always live on in another's heart."

Cicero

Acknowledgments

This book primarily emerged from years of listening to stories from people like you. The traveling community is a very unique family and the relationships we form are ones that often last a lifetime. English is my second language and so believe me when I say that I have relied heavily on the editing of my good friends and family to make this book sound like it's not written in crayons. Greg Powell, Tim Malinovsky, and Janell Zimmer did an amazing job proof reading my book over and over again. The cover and name emerged from the creative minds of my lovely wife, Amy and my dear friends Bill, Tom, and Sean. My friend Rick also provided me with all the resources I needed to even start this project and pushed me to get it done.

The inspiration for this book is that we truly live a short life and we need to try to make the best of it. We get too caught up in daily life and too easily lose perspective of the truly important things in life. I want to thank all the hundreds of colleagues over the years whose stories, bad and good, inspired me to try to be a better person by either following their footsteps or avoiding their tracks. Finally, I want to thank my family for their support and love. My two precious boys are the reason I want to better myself and continue growing as a person, not only as a father, but also as a husband to their mother.

ADDITIONAL RESOURCES

I would love to hear back from you and hear your thoughts. Here is my email address; I will try my best to answer all emails as quickly as I can.

FCMBOOK@gmail.com

I also have a blog set up; please feel free to check it out and post any stories or thoughts you might have for others to read. My goal is that this can be a blog where you can vent or perhaps find some sort of support system. We are all in the same boat, so why not help each other out. You can post your stories or perhaps offer some helpful advice to others reaching out.

www.FirstClassMarriageBook.com

52835636R00115

Made in the USA
San Bernardino, CA
10 September 2019